THE NET EFFECT

HOW CYBERADVOCACY IS CHANGING THE POLITICAL LANDSCAPE

THE NET EFFECT

HOW CYBERADVOCACY IS CHANGING THE POLITICAL LANDSCAPE

DANIEL BENNETT AND PAM FIELDING

Foreword by
U.S. Senator John D. Rockefeller IV

e-advocates Press
Merrifield, VA

*To Devon, Jamaica, and all the nation's children
who hold the promise of a renewed democracy.*

© 1999 *e-advocates* Press, Merrifield, VA 22116-2018
ISBN 1-879617-46-3

Contents

Foreword

I s there anyone who believes that technology, and more dramatically, the Internet, has not rapidly changed our world? Is there any company, any teacher, or any reporter who would say that their work has not been affected or even revolutionized by the technological developments of the last few years? We all know, and even see in our everyday lives, that technology is reshaping the way we play, learn, shop, and do business. But as we readily and at times, perhaps, grudgingly acknowledge these obvious changes, there is a growing cybermovement that may ultimately have an even greater impact on our lives and the future of our nation.

The development of public policy is increasingly being influenced by online advocacy, and there can be no question that the Internet revolution holds tremendous promise and tremendous challenges for the future of politics. *The Net Effect* breaks new ground by addressing this change and exploring how electronic communications is affecting the political environment. It looks to the future to see how the Internet can drive policy and politics in new directions. In doing so, it challenges us to think about how the Internet has already changed our political dialogue and about the promises and pitfalls that lie ahead.

One reason I am so intrigued by this subject is because I have been directly involved in cyberadvocacy. In 1995, I joined with a bipartisan group of senators in creating a program to provide deep discounts for wiring America's schools, libraries and rural health care providers to the Internet. The E-Rate, as the program is commonly referred to, was a bipartisan effort, and the political coalition that formed to support it was diverse. But this diverse group was unified around the use of electronic communications, and in doing so, was able to deliver a strong, clear, and consistent message. The E-Rate campaign employed technology—through Internet Web sites and e-mail—to keep the pressure on decision makers to support a program that is so vital to the future of our country. And interestingly, I believe that the act of using technology in this way actually helped to make the case as to why the E-Rate is so necessary. After all, if lawmakers see that the Internet is such a powerful communications tool, they are far more likely to support and expand its availability to all Americans.

Using understandable examples—including discussion of the E-Rate—*The Net Effect* explains how the Internet is changing our political debates and how groups that understand this emerging technology are gaining a new, stronger voice. The book makes it clear that it is vital that we not let a limited few manipulate the Internet to promote their particular views, and instead seek to harness the power and accessibility of this new technology for everyone.

Really, the future of the Internet depends on this goal being achieved. The Internet could be a remarkable equalizer—giving people in every part of our country access to the same resources and opportunities. This is why a program like the E-Rate, which targets poor and rural communities, is so necessary. Limiting Internet access or control could end up turning technology into yet another barrier to groups that already must struggle to get their voice heard in our society.

As a Senator from the rural state of West Virginia, I am thrilled about the enormous potential for the Internet to help overcome historic geographic barriers. In 1999, West Virginia had among the lowest residential household connectivity rates in the nation. Luckily, our state is a leader in connecting our public institutions like schools and libraries, so that individuals without access in their homes have some exposure and access to technology.

Providing access to the Internet is only a first step toward maximizing its potential. We've got to see to it that advanced technologies are deployed in every part of the country. Our goal should be to use communications technology as a way to bring people together—and that can only really be effectively accomplished if new and cutting-edge developments are available equally in metropolitan areas and mountain towns.

In public institutions such as schools and libraries, it is also important that we educate people on the use and potential of technology. People need to understand the power and influence of the Internet and technology in order to be heard in future debates and to participate in the new electronic economy. And those on the other side of the policy debates— the decision makers—must understand the new dynamics of the Internet. We need to thoughtfully consider how it is used, and try to encourage broad participation, rather than skillful manipulation by only a few.

Personally, I have made the transition from never using e-mail to relying daily on the Internet. From chatting online with students, to reading West Virginia newspaper Web sites, to keeping in touch with friends and associates through e-mail, the Internet is helping me to keep in closer contact with those I represent. It is clear to me that electronic communications, if thoughtfully used and understood, can enhance our political dialogue, promote involvement in the political process and provide an invaluable resource for people who want to know more about the activities of their leaders. The challenge, as discussed in *The Net Effect*, will be to determine how to best harness the power of the Internet to promote more educated and inclusive public debates.

Technology is firmly entrenched as a critical part of our economy, our education system, and now, our political world. Like radio and television before it, the Internet has the potential to dramatically change political campaigns and policy debates. It is up to all of us to make sure that this change is for the better.

U.S. Senator John D. Rockefeller IV
Co-Chairman and Co-Founder,
Forum on Technology and Innovation

Acknowledgments

This book never would have been published were it not for the inspiration and encouragement of our colleagues, the love and faith of our family and friends — and the groundbreaking work of cyberpioneers who came before us.

We are especially grateful to Bob Hansan, President of Capitol Advantage, who envisioned *The Net Effect* even before the authors. His commitment to our work, online and off, made this book and our dream of an Internet advocacy consulting firm possible.

Thanks to our parents, Ricardo and Eleanor Zappone, and Arnold and Nancy Bennett, who taught us by their own examples the importance of participating in democracy and fighting for what you believe in.

And from Pam:

Thanks to my husband, David, and the love of our lives, Devon Kelsey, who make every moment of my life worthwhile.

Diana Faulkner, my sister and friend, thank you for believing in me when I could not, and promising me refuge if I failed on this journey. This book would not have been written were it not for you. Love and thanks, too, to Eleanor, Mark, Peter, Dave, Michael, and Jamie. You are a constant source of love and inspiration.

To my friends at the National Education Association, especially Jerry Byrd and Mary Elizabeth Teasley, thank you for teaching me so much about leadership, politics, and friendship. And to my friends, Brad Cady, Dorie Eger, and Emad and Bahareh Sharghi, thanks for being there all these years.

And from Daniel:

A thanks to my great love Natasha and to Jamaica. You are my constant encouragement, my inspiration and have made all the difference in my life. And you have made Indiana my favorite state to visit. And to Jeremiah, my brother, your warmth and support meant a great deal not only during the writing of this book, but always. And Doris Derrickson, my grandmother, who has helped me out over the years. Your love and support have made the difference in all my endeavors.

A special thanks to my friends at the most dynamic and exciting congressional office, especially Karen Chapman, John Flaherty and Eric Olson who put up with me for years and more. And most of all, my great respect and admiration of Rep. Anna Eshoo, a great and caring leader, who taught me how important it is to always put others before yourself.

And to Scott Cooper, Jeff Kirsch, Doug Bailey and many others who helped me through the writing process.

We are thankful to the many great thinkers and Internet pioneers who allowed us to interview them for this book: John Aravosis, Doug Bailey, Dr. Gary Bass, Jon Bernstein, Joan Blades, Carolyn Breedlove, Wes Boyd, Penny Crowley, Steve Dasbach, Laura Dove, Kathleen deLaski, Ken Deutsch, Rep. Anna Eshoo, Bob Hansan, Roger Hedgecock, Steve Katsanos, Bob Kearney, Jeff Kirsch, Patrick Lemmon, John McMullen, Area Madaras, Phil Noble, Kevin Rooney, Rep. Bobby Rush, Jonah Seiger, James Smith, Mitchelle Stephenson, Lisa Todorovich, Ryan Turner, Peter Weiss, and Mark West. There are several others who we interviewed on background whose information was invaluable.

Thank you to our editors, Jack Hansan, John Kohut and Tim Yoder, and the graphics and production staff, Dan Corbin, Rick Mott, Jim McDonald and Amy Radabaugh who gently steered the production of this book and helped to make it something we could all be proud of.

We are eternally grateful to our colleagues and friends, who gave their time to review this book or share their insights with us: Doug Bailey, Arnold and Nancy Bennett, Barkley Kern, Phil Noble, Barbara Pryor, Kevin Rooney, Sherry Stanley, Roger Stone, Jim Thompson, and Mark West.

While it would have been impossible to write this book without the help of those mentioned, any shortcomings you may find in this work are certainly our own. On all counts, thanks to all those we have mentioned and the millions of budding cyberadvocates.

Chapter 1   Introduction

B ringing change to society is a lot like pushing a boulder up a mountain. Both are challenges made easier by applying technology or people power to the job. Today, Internet technology is making it easier for ordinary citizens to push their boulders—their political agendas—up the steep inclines of our democracy. The "Net effect" is engaging more people in our political process and, in so doing, changing the political landscape.

This book is the story of cybercitizens and Internet pioneers who are traversing this new political landscape and extending the boundaries of politics into cyberspace. Their success in advancing issues, influencing legislation, and turning back federal regulations illustrate why no citizen, interest group, or politician can afford to ignore the potential of the Internet.

Throughout history, political pioneers have paved the way for democratic change and propelled the work of other leaders. Henry David Thoreau pioneered the political tactic of disobeying civil authority in protest of government action. He refused to pay a poll tax to show his opposition to America's war with Mexico, an act of civil disobedience that landed him in jail. Thoreau's action and his essay about it, "Civil Disobedience," influenced two of the

1

most important and successful movements of this century: the non-violent campaign for India's independence led by Mahatma Gandhi; and the civil rights movement inspired by Rosa Parks' refusal to give a white man her seat on a public bus in Montgomery, Alabama. *The Net Effect* examines the efforts of our emerging cyberpolitical pioneers. The book offers their examples as a compass to guide future movements and their leaders.

To realize the potential of the Internet as a tool for political activism, it is important to understand the medium. The Net is like the proverbial elephant that arrived by ship for inspection by the king's wise men. Depending on where one touches it, it is possible to get an entirely different impression. Touching an elephant's ear explains little about the animal's power. Touching an elephant's trunk tells nothing about its size. The Internet, like an elephant, defies quick analysis and simple definition. When misused, it can turn on its handler. And, unlike its four legged counterpart, the Internet grows new parts every day.

The Net Effect's pages recount the personal experiences and stories of those who have inspected the elephant at close range. These accounts present a more complete picture of what the Internet is and can become: a home for pioneering activists, a venue for a new brand of interactive journalism, a virtual district office for legislators, a soap box for interest groups, a citizen action center for constituents, a polling place for voters, an online headquarters for candidates and their campaigns, and a new technology-based political industry.

The evolution of the Internet as a political tool began with Net citizens' promotion of issues directly related to the use and regulation of the technology. Internet censorship and unsolicited e-mail were two of the earliest and most prominent political issues advanced online. As the Internet audience grew, so too did online activism on a more broadly defined set of issues. Several important breakthroughs occurred that helped to establish the Internet as a tool for politics. In 1996, for example, U.S. Senator Bob Dole became the first presidential candidate to announce his campaign's Web site address in a nationally broadcast presidential debate. Despite these early endorsements, the relatively small number of people connected to the Internet limited the medium's potential to transform politics or effect the body politic.

President Clinton's impeachment trial coincided with the maturity of the Internet into a mass medium. The Internet connected a significant and growing cross section of the country: by 1998, one in three American adults were using the Internet. As Chapter 2 reveals, the release of the Starr report on the World Wide Web, like no other cyberevent preceding it, piqued the interests of these Internet users and launched record numbers of citizens into cyberspace. On the day of the report's release, traffic on the Internet reached record highs. As the usage logs would later show, the Internet had achieved critical mass and shown itself to be a potent political tool.

As the impeachment battle demonstrated, the basis of any political movement is an issue. The heart of a successful campaign is a message, one that is carefully framed to stir the passions of its targeted audience. In Chapter 3, we follow in the footsteps of the cybercampaign "Censure and Move On." This campaign demonstrated that a well crafted message and the right technology can turn a massive—yet often passive—Internet audience into activists for a cause. It revealed how technology could be used to leverage the small efforts of activists into a major campaign. But like most successful grassroots actions, the cybertools employed in the campaign would have been useless had the message failed to strike a chord with a significant number of people.

The impeachment process also demonstrated another effect of the Internet on society: It is rapidly transforming other mass media. In Chapter 4, we chart the successful transition of Roger Hedgecock from politician-turned radio talk show host into the leader of an online army. The story illustrates how a local radio broadcaster can have national reach—with the blink of a cursor and at modest cost—courtesy of the power of the Internet. Like the actors who successfully transitioned from silent movies to talkies, radio and television show hosts—and their industries—must learn to adapt to changing technologies. Individuals and organizations that rely on mass media to advance their issues must also learn to leverage these adapted technologies for maximum impact.

Among the leading players who are advancing the Internet as a tool for politics are a new hybrid of cyberpolitical entrepreneurs. The technologies and services developed by these corporate pioneers have helped countless people to communicate with their elected leaders and reconnected voters to the electoral process. Chapter 5 highlights the work of several of the key people who have one eye on the future of the medium and the other on the corporate bottom line. Their success illustrates the emergence of a new cyberpolitical industry. And the strategic vision of these cyberpioneers points to the future of Internet democracy.

Organizations interested in moving an agenda in the Digital Age must make a serious resource commitment to online organizing. A campaign like "Censure and Move On" demonstrated it is possible to launch a "flash campaign" that generates results; however, few cybersavvy organizations would want to leave their agendas to chance. In Chapter 6, we present four compelling case studies that detail the efforts of established organizations, large coalitions, and a political party to embrace cyberadvocacy. These examples illustrate the importance of preparing a plan, devoting resources to the project, and recruiting an online community to meet the overall objectives of the campaign or the organization—for the long haul.

In Chapter 7, we chronicle the work of John Aravosis, a cybersavvy and passionate activist who has battled—and won—a series of one man campaigns against a large corporation, a branch of the military, and even a major publisher of dictionaries. From his apartment in Northwest Washington, D.C., Aravosis has achieved successes worthy of any large high powered public relations firm. His efforts demonstrate that someone with real passion for an issue, a strong message, good timing, and the right tools, can leverage significant change. But empowerment is not reserved for the lone rangers. It is the domain of anyone and any organization that is willing to move boldly into cyberspace.

Elected officials have not yet caught up with their constituents in embracing the Digital Age. During the impeachment process, an avalanche of incoming constituent e-mail overwhelmed congressional staff and their offices' prescribed methods for responding to constituent mail. As more and more citizens turn to the Internet as a tool for communicating with Congress, governors, and state legislators, it is increasingly clear that the savvy elected leader will learn to embrace and communicate in cyberspace. Chapter 8 outlines the scope of this challenge and the risk to elected officials who fail to heed their cyberconstituents' call.

Beyond constituent communication tools, the Internet has given voters, for the first time and in one place, instant access to a wealth of information about candidates for elected office. With a few clicks of a mouse, voters can access candidates' voting records, Federal Election Commission reports on campaign contributions, position statements and more. In Chapter 9, we explore the work of DemocracyNet, a pioneering organization that uses its Web site to provide voters and other users with critical resources to make election day decisions and enable all candidates to campaign on a level playing field. Savvy candidates must recognize that the Internet—and operations like DemocracyNet—are now a vital element of any winning campaign.

In Chapter 10, we look at the elements of a cyberadvocacy program and offer the reader some specific suggestions and tools to begin advocating in cyberspace. Even as this book is published, Internet advocacy is helping to move our democracy and public policy in new directions. Those who learn to leverage the medium will help determine this course.

The stories presented in these pages chronicle an important—but limited—period in the history of the Internet, specifically the Net's coming of age as a tool for political activism. We were among the direct participants in this process, and actively worked to stretch the boundaries of what was possible. This book is based on our own personal observations, interviews with most of the principals, contemporaneous news stories, and the few studies that have been done in this area. The Net Effect is our tribute to the cybercitizens and pioneers who have made the vision of Internet democracy a reality and our contribution to all those who desire to advance their agendas in a Digital Age.

Chapter 2

Caught in the Net: A New Mass Medium

Storming the Castle

Armed guards were stationed around the printing presses as copies of the Independent Counsel's Report on the Impeachment (Starr report) were churned out. The House of Representatives had demanded maximum security during the printing operation. The Government Printing Office (GPO) was printing the Starr report, and House leadership saw it as a historic document ranking with the Warren Committee Report on the Kennedy Assassination, the Watergate materials, and the Iran-Contra materials.[1] After all, this report concerned the most significant political occurrence possible in American political history, the potential removal from office of a President of the United States. Thousands of copies of the Starr report rolled off the presses well protected from any disruption or theft from the outside. These

---

[1] "We had a strict requirement from the House of Representatives to have the utmost security practice while we printed the publication. So as a result we had armed police officers stationed at key production points throughout the plant, including right here in the pressroom. And in terms of the other publications we've had, such as the Warren Report on the Kennedy Assassination, the Watergate materials, the Iran-Contra materials, certainly it ranks up there with those publications." Andy Sherman spokesman for the GPO, *Weekend All Things Considered*, Feb 13, 1999.

copies were destined for delivery to Congress and for sale to the American public at Government Printing Office retail stores.

Later, escorted by police officers, government couriers hand delivered printed copies of the Starr report to each congressional office. This document began the awesome process of impeachment; a process that would end as members of Congress cast a vote that would rock the nation and exercise a power granted the Congress as a last resort against tyranny.

The Independent Counsel, Judge Kenneth Starr, had spent four long years investigating the President. In January 1998, he had found damaging allegations against the President that he would argue were the high crimes and misdemeanors that should trigger impeachment. But several months passed before Judge Starr issued his report, during which the news media spent endless hours speculating about what Starr had uncovered, mobbing the courthouse where he conducted the grand jury proceedings, and staking out the residences and hotel rooms of each of the people involved in the investigation. The main question was: Would Starr's report include allegations and evidence that would bring down the presidency?

Once the Office of the Independent Counsel indicated that the report was ready to be sent to Congress, the House leadership was sensitive to the need to follow the rules closely as the impeachment process began. And Starr and the House leadership were cognizant of the heavy media coverage of the unfolding drama. Unlike the usual transporting of government documents between buildings, there was great fanfare in the delivery of the Starr report. Vans packed with boxes pulled up on the parking lot of the Capitol building. With cameras rolling, the Sergeant at Arms of the U.S. House of Representatives took the boxes from the vans that had come from the Office of the Independent Counsel, while uniformed Capitol Police kept watch, the Sergeant at Arms locked the boxes behind heavy wooden doors to wait until rules regarding their distribution had been voted on.

The Republican House Leadership, knowing that the contents of the report were deeply embarrassing to the Democratic President, insisted on as open a process as possible, and the House of Representatives voted to make the report available to as wide an audience as possible, and with great haste.[2] In addition to reprinting the document as is normal with public documents, the House leadership decided to release an electronic version of the report through the Thomas Web site,[3] the Library of Congress's main repository for legislative documents.

Despite the pomp and circumstance surrounding the printing and delivery of the printed version, an effort that would have once been vital for the orderly distribution of a document, it would soon become obvious that the Internet had made the paper delivery process nearly obsolete. The distribution of the electronic version of the Starr report was available hours before the printed copies and in quantities that far surpassed the number that would be printed. Thirty (or even three) years ago, the thousands of printed copies would have been the primary means of release for the report. But now, just a few years into the Digital Age, the Starr report flowed like water

---

[2] H. Res. 525-A resolution providing for a deliberative review by the Committee on the Judiciary of a communication from an Independent Counsel, and for the release thereof, and for other purposes.

[3] The report can be found at *thomas.loc.gov/icreport*

over a collapsing dam to millions of citizens across the
country in just a few hours.

In just a few years the Internet had been transformed from a
little used electronic network to a mass medium rivaling the
reach of all the other media. And the Internet had built-in
characteristics that allowed it to out pace television, provide
more in-depth coverage than newspapers, out talk "talk
radio", and scoop major magazines. And with the release of
the Starr report, the Internet had become a primary means for
the U.S. Government to release documents to the public, less
dramatic but infinitely faster than the carefully guarded
books. Politicians and the media were talking about history
being made that day, but the more enduring and significant
change was that the Internet and politics were now forever
bound together.

The early release of the Starr report was due to the hard work
of a few young Internet pioneers. The change from old to new
media is never a smooth process. There are no rules or
handbooks to guide the pioneers who create new techniques
to suit a new medium. These pioneers are often energetic,
young, savvy professionals who are out to prove the tried and
true methods are now archaic. And in 1998, a few young
people made their mark by using the Internet technology and
quick thinking to help get the Starr report out to the public.

Potentially, any individual can quickly become a powerful
publisher; potentially, any organization can instantaneously
mount a mass movement. But to achieve these feats of near
magic, there have to be people who understand the capabilities of the technology—or at least know how to hire people
who do.

A Few Young Geeks

"No, thank you." It was a polite response to the offer made by
Laura Dove, staff person with the Senate Republican Conference. But it was not the right response to what turned out to
be a phenomenal opportunity. Laura Dove had been calling
reporters and news desks offering a two or three hour lead at
getting the Starr report, and at least one news desk editor
refused the offer. Why would any news outlet turn this down?
Because they simply did not understand the offer, and because they did not understand the dynamics of information
distribution on the Web.

When the House voted to make the report public and the
House leadership decided to electronically publish the report,
they received an electronic file from the Office of the Independent Counsel. Members of Congress were to get a paper
version just prior to the public release—and they would also
be able to access the report from a Web page accessible to
offices within the House of Representatives.

The House had set up a process by which the Starr report,
which had been under lock and key, would become public.
The Office of the Independent Counsel worked with the Clerk
of the House's office and the Committees on Judiciary and
House Administration (then called the House Committee on
House Oversight) to decipher the report, a WordPerfect
document originally, and convert it into formats appropriate
for printing and for posting on the Web.

The printed version of the Starr report, like any other official
document, is treated as the official version. The electronic
version, especially when on a Web site, is treated as an

inexact copy for many reasons.[4] Being an official version, the Government Printing Office quickly set the presses to print copies with the intentionally dramatic and unusual presence of armed guards. The process by which the electronic version was created and transported was much less formal and without additional security that is normal for House offices.

The Clerk of the House made the electronic version for distribution. That version was produced on CD-ROM, a CD (compact disc) that holds electronic data. CD-ROM copies of the report were hand delivered to the Library of Congress and the House Press Gallery. Because CD-ROMs are physical objects they could not be delivered electronically. They had to be physically transported to their intended recipients, just like paper copies. The CD-ROM was intended to be an accurate copy of the official document. Unlike most electronically delivered documents, but like bound paper copies, the CD-ROMs could not be easily changed. The mechanics of this distribution were counter intuitive to an Internet-aware person like Laura Dove.

The Web is a new medium that does not fit into the neat categories of earlier media. And it doesn't work in the halls of Congress the way newspapers, radio stations, and television do. The established journalists have press passes and can ride an elevator reserved for themselves and members of Congress to the press gallery. Various journalists can pigeonhole a Member and perhaps get the inside scoop. But Dove, who herself once worked for an online political news site, knew of a very different type of journalist. Working with James Smith,

---

[4] Web pages are not the same as paper pages, so usually page number references that are based on printing on a set paper size do not correspond to most electronic versions. Also the officially printed version is less susceptible to alteration.

a very proficient Web technology expert in the House Majority Whip's office, and some other staffers, she helped to set up a super fast distribution plan for the hottest document to hit the town in decades.

It was this CD-ROM version that the news desk chief had been expecting when Laura Dove called and offered her unofficial version. The more official electronic copy, hot off the press— actually a CD burner—was to be delivered to the press gallery. And eventually it probably showed up, but not until several hours after Smith and Dove had already electronically distributed their unofficial version. From within the House they copied the version from the House internal Web site where the report was initially posted for House offices only. Of course, that version was easily reproducible. Smith digitally compressed it to make it smaller and more easily e-mailed or downloaded. Many other House offices were similarly making printed copies for internal consumption and perhaps to distribute to others. The House had no rules for redistributing the report once an office had officially received it in electronic or in paper form.

Then, for those journalists who showed interest in receiving the much anticipated document, the compressed copy was e-mailed or FTP'ed to two or three dozen major news outlets. ("FTP'ed" is colloquial for using an Internet program that allows efficient movement of files over the Internet.) Within minutes the world had access to the report, waiting no longer than most members of Congress had. And it was this copy that the House Press Gallery had on its computer system.

No rules or laws had been broken.[5] It was merely a question of procedure, of whether old notions of how to distribute information are valid anymore. Smith and Dove had made themselves more valuable to journalists by providing this favor, one of the most important jobs in congressional offices. It didn't change the general story; it was not a "leak." But in the age of the Internet, speed counts and there are no longer any excuses for delays in distributing information. And, because the Internet is immediate, any other method of distribution is a form of delay.

Congress is filled with young staffers, and when you ask them "Paper or e-mail?" the answer for most of them is: "What's paper?" For the older members of Congress, this was revolutionary. But in voting to release the report unedited over the Internet they had done something quite revolutionary. And Smith and Dove had given the country two additional hours to read the report for itself before the nightly news and morning newspapers put their own spin on the meaning of the Starr report.

Dash/Dot/Dash

"What Hath God Wrought!" telegraphed Samuel F. B. Morse over a hundred and fifty years before the electronic release of the Starr report. Morse had used transcendent language to describe the telegraph in the first publicly sent electronic message. From within the Capitol, a building representing the aspirations of a free people to govern themselves, Morse had started a communications revolution. This new technology was intended to empower the people to better their society.

---

[5] Laura Dove was probably one of the most rules conscious people in the Senate, her father being the Senate's Parliamentarian (the official in charge of the rules of the Senate).

Samuel F. B. Morse's invention of the telegraph directly presaged the creation—a century later—of the Internet.[6] The shape of Morse's medium was determined both by its strengths and its limitations. Essentially, the telegraph was an on-off switch that could be operated at a great distance, producing clicks of various lengths. Morse helped turn those clicks into the standardized alphabet of long and short clicks we know as Morse code.

Dot/dash was A. Dash/dot/dot/dot was B. Three short clicks made an S, three long clicks an O. Thus, dot/dot/dot • dash dash/dash • dot/dot/dot is the SOS that became an international distress call. Dot/dot/dot/dash, the four notes at the heart of Beethoven's Fifth Symphony, became V, the signal of Victory during the Second World War.[7]

Morse code required skilled operators to send and receive messages. It would never become the medium of the ordinary citizen. But Alexander Graham Bell's invention, the telephone, provided the ease of use that allowed ordinary citizens to adopt an electronic communication technology. With the advent of radio and television, electronic media could become mass media, but—unlike the telephone—these mass media were not interactive.

Electronic communication has played a huge role in American politics. From the radio propaganda of Father Charles E. Coughlin and President Franklin D. Roosevelt's fireside chats in the 1930s to Richard M. Nixon's televised "Checkers"

[6] Tom Standage, *The Victorian Internet* (Walker and Company, New York, 1998).

[7] *www.futurenet.com/classicalnet/reference/works/b/beethoven-sym5.html*

speech September 23, 1952, politicians made use of the pervasive reach of technology to talk directly to the population. In this same way, the release of the Starr report signaled the coming of age of a new technology that is going to play a commanding role in politics. Communication is the vehicle of politics and the Internet is the most powerful political vehicle yet built.

The Internet is a network of connected computers, allowing users to read, listen, write, and talk between any computers on that network. The two computer applications that are the most compelling for average users are e-mail and the World Wide Web. Sending and receiving e-mail is quickly replacing written personal correspondence and paper memoranda. And the Web is replacing the printing press.

The Internet was born out of a project to connect major computer centers around the United States. Conceived as an interlocking network of connections that would continue to function even if some of the connections failed, the network was first called ARPANET after the Defense Advanced Research Projects Agency (DARPA).[8] Several applications were developed that allowed the users on the networked computers to use any other computer on the network. But the network started between computers that were not generally available to the public and the applications and the computers took training to use. It was not until many advances had been made and there existed a wider distribution of personal computers in the eighties that the Internet became a huge phenomenon.

---

[8] *www.darpa.mil*

One Internet application that made the final and most compelling reason for the Internet to explode was the "Web browser." In 1991, Tim Berners-Lee created the World Wide Web as a way to allow scientists at CERN, the European Laboratory for Particle Physics, to connect the overwhelming number of scientific papers, reports, and projects scattered on all the computers. He created a new document format that everyone could view through one computer program that would be available to all. And he developed a new computer protocol that allowed people to get access to those documents on computers other than their own without their own computer being similar to the one being accessed and without needing any prior authority to gain access.

The Web has evolved quickly into an engine of new commercial growth and openness in elections and government. The Web and the underlying Internet protocols are swallowing whole other technologies—television, telephony, radio, newspapers and other print media—and becoming a vast international bazaar of commercial transactions. The immediacy of television and radio have been echoed by the development of streaming technologies, which allow audio and video programs to be simulcast on computers in real time. In some cases the Web has been able to replace uses of other technologies, but in all cases it has radically changed the use and perception of other technologies.

The Web has become a medium that defies easy description both because it seems to be an amalgamation of all the other media and because it is still in a state of radical development. And there are almost no limits to who can publish and who can receive information: the cost is low and decreasing hourly; technology is allowing better and faster access; and governmental restrictions are very difficult to enforce.

The very nature of information has changed. Consider an electronic document that is found at an official government Web site. Is it as valid as a printed original? Or is the printed version just a copy? And something posted to the Internet can be seen by anyone and usually can be copied and perpetuated forever. The Internet has changed the nature of communication, and it will take many years for society to come to terms with all of these implications.

As most people realize, documents are now normally composed on computers. Then they are printed. But it is now possible to quickly distribute an electronic version directly to the audience, without printing, binding and shipping. And, unlike a printed and bound document, the electronic format gives the reader greater control over the document. The reader can decide what parts of the document to print out, if any. In the case of the Starr report, many readers simply used the search tools built into most Web browsers to get them past the boring stuff into the more prurient parts.

Have You Left No Sense of Decency

While Congress was deciding to release an unfiltered version of the Starr report to the public, the House Commerce Committee was discussing how to block commercial pornography from children using the Internet. Congressman Bobby Rush (D-IL), co-founder of the Chicago chapter of the Black Panther Party, scolded the other Members sitting at the dais in the hearing room for what he perceived as gross hypocrisy. His words echoed Counsel for the Army Joseph Welch's plaintive "At long last, have you left no sense of decency?" during the McCarthy hearings in an earlier era.

Rush had watched members of Congress authorize the largest distribution of any Internet document for release that same day, an official government document filled with salacious details that were sexually explicit. Later, in an interview, Rush reflected on the jarring disassociation of the actions and the words of his colleagues. "I sincerely believe that the release of the Starr report on the Internet was strictly political. The decision had no sensitivity, no concern, no interest in the impact of the Starr report in particular in its pornographic disclosures on the minds and attitudes and the mental well-being of children."

The referral of the Independent Counsel for impeachment was shocking in its political content and constitutional implications and in the sexual nature of the material it contained. Shocking in that it was freely distributed to such a huge audience despite the concern many members of Congress had about others publishing similarly sexually explicit material.

However, the report referred only to sexual situations that involved the President, and some members of Congress strongly believed that those actions must be discussed as a matter of public record in a public impeachment trial. House Judiciary Committee Chairman Henry Hyde (R-IL) stated, "This referral belongs to the American people, and they have a right to know its contents. The American people have patiently waited as rumors and speculation have substituted for facts and information. It is time that we move this process ahead, and the public release of the referral will help us embark on that process." [9]

---

[9] United States House of Representatives Committee on the Judiciary News Release: September 10, 1998.

It shocked the sensibilities of Congressman Rush and others who wondered how a document that detailed sexual acts would be released by the government unfiltered. It did not seem necessary to him for the document, no matter how important, to include such details. It seemed ironic that Congress passed the legislation that would ultimately make it illegal for commercial firms to do exactly what Congress had done.

On most of the government sites, including Thomas, there were no warnings or filtering enabling technology used. Once having made the decision to release the report as received, there could be no editorial comments added. So the report was released unadulterated, so to speak. However, unlike the government sites, most of the media sites included some type of warning or description of the tone of the content. On the other hand, the expectation that there would be sexual content obviously increased the volume and number of viewers to begin with.

The Report Heard Around the World Wide Web

Millions of people knew that the Starr report was going to be released and were searching the Web for a copy. Unlike television signals broadcast to everyone, without direct connections, a Web site must be logged into on a one-to-one connection. Although the network protocol that the Web uses to allow for logging on is very efficient, the computers (known as servers when used for the Web) and their connections do have limits to the traffic they can handle.

Sites were pummeled. The Library of Congress, anticipating the huge amount of traffic, set up methods to reduce the likelihood of total meltdown. Media sites also hunkered down for the explosion. "People moved from site to site [in order to see whether a site had the report]," said Lisa Todorovich of the *Washingtonpost.com* site. A single person can easily visit and revisit a site several times an hour, multiplying the traffic to that site.

By getting the report earlier by way of Smith and Dove, sites such as *Washingtonpost.com* were able to satisfy their viewers and decrease the multiple visits. Of course, having people download a document is a strain on resources. But it is a good problem for a commercial site, because it means that they are useful to viewers and ultimately get more traffic. The more viewers, the higher the potential for advertising revenue.

On the day the Starr report was released, America Online (AOL), which at the time had over sixteen million subscribers, had its biggest day ever. According to AOL's Kathleen deLaski, AOL had its first 10 million user-hour day. AOL recorded over 800,000 downloads of the report in the first 24 hours.

AOL put the report front and center on the screen as soon as a member logged onto the service. This made it easier for those who just wanted to download the report and AOL avoided many unnecessary searches.

AOL, *Washingtonpost.com* and other commercial sources of the Starr report struggled to meet demand. Most of the major media sites on the Internet were tough to get into because of the heavy traffic. However, despite the load, persistent viewers could expect to get their own copy fairly easily and quickly.

The usual home page of the Library of Congress's Thomas Web site was moved to allow for a stripped down Web page that pointed to the former home page and to the Starr report. Another Web server (a computer dedicated to displaying a Web site) was set up just to handle the hundreds of thousands of downloads requested. Once the Library of Congress received the official CD-ROM version it was loaded onto the server. It is likely that the strain of the millions of visitors would have been much worse if the commercial sites hadn't been there to help. Fortunately, the system held up under the strain. It was tough going for viewers, but not impossible. The report was out.

A New Player in Town

The next day some of the major newspapers printed the Starr report in their daily editions. *The New York Times* even published it in book form. While the sales of the book were huge, the volume and speed of the Internet version outstripped the printed book. The Web was the new guy on the block and had made its presence known. The other media still had greater total penetration, but the Internet was up there with the biggest of them.

It was the "Drudge Report," an Internet-only news site, which first broke the Monica Lewinsky story that began the impeachment process. The Internet was an integral part of the unfolding of the scandal. With the release of the Starr report, the Internet had shown its huge growth and importance as a news media.

The rise in influence of the Internet as a news media contributed to making the Web sites of major media equal partners with their "mother ship." *The Washington Post* newspaper depended on its Internet section, *Washingtonpost.com*, to get the Starr report. Because James Smith and Laura Dove electronically released the report, Lisa Todorovich had been able to quickly get a copy for *The Washington Post*. Todorovich was one of the new Internet savvy journalists who would not turn down the opportunity to receive information by e-mail. It was Todorovich's copy of the Starr report that allowed the editors from the newspaper section to check the document and allow it to be posted to the Internet—and to be printed in the newspaper the following morning. In a sense, the newspaper version played second fiddle to the Web site by trailing in terms of readership and timeliness.

The Washington Post had been a major player in the last impeachment crisis, when it broke the story of President Richard Nixon's involvement in Watergate. During this impeachment, it would be the Internet section that would help bring the information to the public. And *Newsweek*, a magazine produced by the Washington Post Company, had actually been involved in investigating the story that would lead to the Starr report. But this time it would be a much smaller organization that would break the story—on the Internet.

Matt Drudge's eponymous "Drudge Report" broke the story. Drudge is known for breaking many things: journalistic conventions, rumors, new ground, and—some allege—ethics. But Drudge represents the art of what's possible with the advent of the Web. The "Drudge Report" exists only in cyberspace and is obtainable for free to everyone with access to the Internet. It is essentially a one man operation and initially had no outlet through anything but the Web. He didn't own a press and he didn't own a radio or television tower. But these days, anyone can set up a Web site cheaply (or for free), and that Web site is instantly viewable by tens of millions.

The speed, the wide coverage, the ease of use, and huge amount of information contained on the Internet has created the opportunity for the death of privacy. This new medium, more than all the others combined, has accelerated the disappearance of secrets. At its core, news is about getting the stories out. Now it is harder and harder to contain a story.

A Brave New World Wide Webbed

There is a theory that civilization drastically changes around the time of major innovations in information technology: the printing press, radio, television, etc. These changes have included the ability to form new types of governing institutions, the rapid improvements in the ability to conduct trade, and shifts in every other social interaction. The release of the Starr report suggests that the Internet has begun to alter our political landscape.

The Internet was originally designed to connect computers together to allow remote computing. The success of the personal computer for use in offices for word processing led to a snowballing effect where now 40 percent of American households have computers. Networked together, these computers have created a system much greater than could previously have been imagined.

The Starr report's release is likely to be seen as more historical than its content. The impeachment referral moved the process forward, but it did not move the American public to demand the removal of the President. And ultimately the report was rejected officially by the Senate.

The release—as opposed to the report that was released—accomplished much more. It definitively showed that nothing can be kept secret, that nothing can successfully filter information from the public, that government documents are owned by everyone, that everything can be communicated instantly, and that everyone can be a publisher and receiver of information.

Within a year of the Starr report release, Congressman Christopher Cox (R-CA) released a report on the Internet related to the intrigue over Chinese espionage and acquisition of high technology from the United States.[10] The report was produced especially for the Web with much greater effort in the presentation than the rather plain presentation of the Starr report. And the report had been edited for national security reasons, mainly to keep the means of obtaining the information secret. Now cognizant of the power of the Internet as a distribution channel, members of Congress have become much better equipped to produce Internet documents for public consumption.

---

[10] *www.house.gov/coxreport*

Chapter 3 Flying Toasters and Five Minute Activists

Censure and Move On

The release of the Starr report and the impeachment hearings produced a great deal of public interest. According to the polls, most people disagreed with Congress's actions to proceed with the impeachment process. But widespread disagreement with congressional action will not in itself sway Congress to change its actions. Several groups and many individuals organized to pressure Congress to stop the impeachment.

After more than eight months of constant talk of impeachment, Wes Boyd and Joan Blades were fed up with Washington politics. They felt disconnected from the process, and they believed that the vast majority of the public was too. Congress was likely to have a long drawn out impeachment trial, despite the fact that the relevant facts had already been established. Boyd and Blades believed what the President had done was wrong, but felt it did not rise to the level of an impeachable offense. They decided to try and get the Congress to stop the impeachment process. And to make this happen there would need to be a concerted movement from constituents to get a majority of Congress to focus on what Boyd and Blades believed a majority of citizens wanted.

Boyd, Blades and a few others decided to organize an Internet based advocacy campaign. Their plan was to rely on the Internet to help channel public dissatisfaction with the impeachment process into a well coordinated cybercampaign. Their campaign, "Censure and Move On," was the largest and most concerted of all the groups acting against the President's impeachment. Their success in organizing grassroots action was due, in large part, to their unique understanding of how people use computers.

Warm and Fuzzy Computers

Boyd and Blades first made their mark in computer technology by developing technology that is about inactivity, screen savers. The company they founded in 1987, Berkeley Systems, became profitable based on the success of screen saver software.[1] Screen savers protect computer monitors from having an image burn into the screen by automatically blanking out (the screen goes dark) or being replaced by constantly moving images. In other words, the more inactive the computer user, the more necessary the program was.

The Berkeley Systems screen saver collection, After Dark, included several whimsical and entertaining animations. Some of the most popular were the flying toasters and a fish aquarium. Computer users could pick out their favorite animation from a wide selection and customize the various options including how many fish were in the aquarium or how burnt the toast in the flying toasters. The basic criteria for buying a screen saver became whether it was entertaining, not how well it worked, because simply blanking the screen was the most effective screen saver. Boyd and Blades had found a

[1] *www.berksys.com/news/bkgd.html*

way that a computer program could be useful, and therefore a necessity, and at the same time an entertainment device. Most people would frown at buying an entertaining word processor or other business oriented software, but if the computer was not being used anyway, the playfulness of a screen saver does not interfere with working. It made choosing a screen saver a matter of personal taste.

Most people use personal computers; and Boyd and Blades demonstrated that the personal computer could be even more personal with the addition of a screen saver. Being able to add a feature that made using the computer amusing and friendly, people would flock to make their otherwise utilitarian object into something that gave them pleasure. Picking odd or beautiful screen savers allowed computer users to express themselves. For many users, their computer had become a warm and fuzzy device. From a distance the computer could look like an aquarium, and if the computer had speakers, sound like one too. The images were mesmerizing, which prompted the computer user to sometimes impatiently wait for the image to appear just so that they could watch it.

Screen savers were everywhere; Berkeley Systems and competing screen savers could often be seen in the background of a newsroom during television news shows. Screen savers are now ubiquitous, in no small part because it is a feature of the Windows and Macintosh operating systems. The use of screen savers is declining as energy saving features that actually turn off the computer monitor are being used. Although computer screen wallpaper and various colored and shaped computer monitors and boxes allow personal computers to feel personal, it was the screen saver that made computers personable.

Wes Boyd and Joan Blades were also early developers of award winning software that made it easier for members of the disabled community to access computers. Starting with a grant from the National Institutes of Health, they developed assistive technology to allow blind and partially sighted people to use personal computers. As the computer changed from a machine being run by specialists to being a mainstream tool, creating assistive technology became a necessity to permit physically challenged people to benefit from the capacity of computers.

In creating software to help people use computers, such as screen savers and assistive programs, Boyd and Blades had helped to tear down the walls that block and alienate people from computers. If computers were to be an important part of people's lives, users would need to feel more comfortable with them. In many cases that entailed people accommodating a computer's characteristics. Since the beginning of personal computers, technology improvements have made them faster and more powerful, allowing the computer hardware and software developers to make computer designs that would better accommodate people. Accommodation is not quite the same as acceptance, and it was the insight of Boyd and Blades to sneak frivolity into an otherwise utilitarian software program that helped soften the image of all computers.

Many years after the popularization of computers and the success of screen savers, the Internet has also drastically changed how computers are viewed. The use of e-mail and surfing the World Wide Web has further taken the hard edges off personal computing. And computers are now sold in candy colored sleek cases, often equipped with speakers and other peripherals designed for entertainment. Game playing on computers, especially since solitaire is included with Windows, is standard. Now that people feel comfortable with computers, they are more likely to use the computer to accomplish various tasks. Retail level electronic commerce is succeeding in large part because people feel comfortable using their computers.

Many people are apolitical, because they don't feel like they can be part of the process. Often this alienation is due to the perceived difficulty in participating politically and how little effect their participation would have. Boyd and Blades took some pages from their earlier efforts that made the computer less alienating and applied it to making the politics more accessible. Their secret ingredient was the computer, now tamed, which would now be the tool they used to make politics friendlier. By using a computer, an individual could participate at their own pace and timetable; clicking a few buttons while surfing the Internet was all that was necessary to be a political participant. By making participation less difficult, Boyd and Blades could move millions to e-mail members of Congress.

Traditionally, people contact their member of Congress to let them know how they feel about particular issues. And many people had been individually contacting Congress in support of and in opposition to impeachment. Boyd and Blades believed that many of the voices that were heard came from people with extreme viewpoints, those who are more likely than others to make that contact. They envisioned creating a mass movement that would resonate with many more people, and bring them into the political process. They set out to create a grassroots campaign and try to shake Congress from what they perceived of its obsession with impeachment.

Organizing a "Flash Campaign"

For any mass movement, whether it happens in cyberspace or on the streets, there are at least two requirements. First and foremost is reaching a large number of people. The second is moving them to action. Usually, accomplishing these two objectives takes considerable planning, coalition building, money, plenty of workers, and time. And any call to action is usually most successful convincing activists and people already committed to the issue. Boyd and Blades endeavored to create a campaign without any of these things. Their target audience was made up of unlikely activists; people who felt alienated by Washington and were relatively nonpolitical. In order to accomplish their objective of having a national campaign, they would have to break new political ground.

They had a few things on their side: their intuition about how people would react to the opportunity to voice their disapproval of the impeachment process; a passion in trying to make politics less alienating and more accessible for disaffected people; and a keen sense of how to use Internet technology to make the campaign possible. They used the term "flash campaign" to help describe the potential power of using the Internet. Just as flash floods come without warning and wreak havoc, their "flash campaign" would strike suddenly and overwhelmingly to astonish Congress and confound the impeachment process.

They were aware of the past Internet grassroots campaigns on various issues that related to technology. They looked into how to set up a Web site that was geared to sending messages to Congress. After some research, they set up a special Web site for the campaign. They adhered to a few guiding principles in its design. The most important was to keep it simple.

First they came up with a simple message and name for their movement: "Censure and Move On." In four words they had encapsulated their feelings regarding the President and the action that they hoped Congress would take. The message was not antagonistic or outrageous. It was designed to reflect a centrist position that they believed a majority of people felt.

They then obtained a Web address that was taken from the name of the campaign and would be easy to remember and possible to guess if you knew the name of the campaign: *www.moveon.org*. Web addresses are normally selected based on the organization that owns the site, but in this case there was no preexisting organization. Finding a good Web address that is available is growing more difficult, because everybody in the world is competing against each other to get the best ones. Nevertheless, Boyd and Blades found a Web address that fit their campaign.

The design of the site was sparse, not loaded down with graphics. Graphics slow down the downloading of a Web page. The focus was on the message and making it as easy as possible to take part in the campaign. Also making it simple meant spending less time and money. And they spent a pittance compared with the cost of setting up phone banks, postage for a mass mailing, buying media advertising and many of the other normal expenditures associated with an organization reaching out to potential participants. The main thrust of the campaign was to send messages to Congress.

They created an online petition that allowed Web site visitors to quickly read the one sentence message, and fill out a simple form that signified agreement with the statement and forwarded the message to Congress. The technology to fill out a form and process it is built into the Web and they used the

information in the form to match a person with a congressional district. Then the site automatically reformatted the
filled-in form into an e-mail that was sent to the appropriate
member of Congress.

Once the site was set up on September 22, Boyd, Blades and
others sent out e-mail to hundreds of people, mainly personal
contacts. They also alerted the media. Within a day the effort
had taken root. According to a press release issued by Blades,
the movement was self building: "Censure and Move On, the
censure petition Web site, officially was launched at 9 AM PST
on September 22. In its first 24 hours the web site collected
506 signatures and added 12 new volunteers to its ranks.
These volunteers will be calling radio stations, writing editors,
and generally spreading the word. By 5 PM today, more than
1500 signatures have been collected altogether, showing
dramatic growth."

The site functioned as a virtual organization, including
updates on its own progress, displaying some of the comments submitted by petitioners, connecting volunteers to
tasks that would help to spread the word and grow the
movement. It was a snowball effect. Within a week, the site
had recorded over one hundred thousand petition signers.
Eventually the campaign would gain around a half million
supporters sending messages to Congress.

Once having reached a large audience, the work of persuading
Congress began. Members of Congress who accepted e-mail
were flooded with individual e-mail generated by "Censure
and Move On."

All the e-mail arrived in congressional offices with the same
message. And because the e-mail were routed based on

congressional districts, congressional offices only received e-mail from their own districts. However, most of the e-mail did not include the full postal address of the petitioner, which is the main way that congressional offices can determine that a message is from the same district if the ZIP code is split between different districts. Also because most offices only respond to messages by sending a response through the U.S. Postal Service, not over the Internet, petitioners who did not include their full address were usually not responded to by the office.

Boyd and Blades also organized using the old fashioned formats for getting the MoveOn message across, in paper copies of the petition, by phone calls and by personal contact, in part because of their perception that not all members of Congress would read or recognize e-mail. Copies of the petition were distributed to each of the congressional offices. In addition to that, volunteers from across the country visited congressional offices in Washington, D.C. and more than half of the district offices that congressmen maintain in their home state. Also, a toll free phone number was set up to allow people to call Congress at no cost.

The novelty and success of the campaign caught the media's attention. General coverage of the impeachment included the reaction of citizens. In part that was covered by polling and by anecdotal "man in the street" interviewing. But the well designed and easily accessed press releases of the "Censure and Move On" campaign site helped to make itself part of the impeachment reaction coverage. Joan Blades acted as the main spokesperson for journalists. A whole section of the site was devoted to media coverage and to helping journalists reach Joan Blades both by phone number and a Web-form on the site. And the stories helped to motivate potential signers to participate as well as amplifying the effect of petitioners. "Censure and Move On" had made a big splash, but the question was did it succeed?

A Measure of Success

As the distribution of the Starr report had shown that the Internet was a mass medium, the "Censure and Move On" campaign demonstrated that the Internet could provide fertile ground for grassroots action. Boyd and Blades had been able to reach thousands of people, most of whom were not political activists. The ease with which viewers of the Web site could sign the petition, the simplicity of the message, and a message that echoed the alienation that many of the signers felt toward Congress, were all aspects that made gaining large numbers possible.

The amount of time that signers had to take to read and sign an Internet petition could be just seconds. Blades described these people as five minute activists, able to follow the news, form an opinion, but not necessarily have the initiative to take time out of a hectic life to write and mail a message to far-away Washington, D.C.

Another effect of the campaign was to help the media find and focus on a significant movement that epitomized the sense of many Americans that the Congress was moving too far. Although the effort entailed in being a participant in the campaign was low, the weight of the overall numbers was significant. Also the story had the added novelty of being an Internet-based grassroots campaign.

During the impeachment process, Congress was battered by an overwhelming response from constituents by phone, fax, town hall participation, letters, and e-mail. The messages reflected a wide response of opinions, from absolute hatred of the President to calls to fire Judge Starr. The "Censure and Move On" campaign was a significant part of that reaction, but not by any means the sole message being heard by Congress. And although there were several other campaigns conducted over the Internet, this one stood out because of its huge number of participants.

The "Censure and Move On" effort's main goal was to stop the impeachment process. However, the impeachment process moved on and did not end until after the President was acquitted by a vote by the Senate. At no point in the process did the Republican majorities in the House and Senate bring a clear vote on a censure resolution. There was no censure, but on the other hand the President was not forced to leave office.

The success of the campaign can be measured as a mixed success. Just getting political participation by large numbers of the public helps invigorate the representational democracy of the country. And the petitions helped to create a backdrop of support for the congressional Democrats who might have appeared as being purely partisan supporters of their President. And it is conceivable that the drumbeat to remove the President would have succeeded if it hadn't been met with discordant messages from concerned citizens arriving through cyberspace. Allowing the President to stay on was a delayed but important victory for the campaign. And it is often the case that the main effect of a grassroots campaign is to set down roots for future battles.

Fast Forward

Boyd and Blades have continued their efforts past the initial campaign. Their new messages are intended to convert the "five minute" activists into more committed activists. Two of the new main efforts include prompting the petitioners to pledge both time and money to political efforts based on the votes of their member of Congress in the impeachment vote and to promote gun control. The pledge campaign would send a message to Congress that people would remember the choices made during their term. Taking up the gun control issue is a sign that Boyd and Blades are interested in other issues and that they believe that their "five minute activists" will move on to other issues as well.

Because all of the petitioners left their e-mail addresses and accepted the possibility that they would be contacted in the future, it was possible for "Censure and Move On" to contact them after the impeachment process was over. The "Censure and Move On" Web site continues to be the virtual headquarters in which the history of the campaign is chronicled and the new efforts are coordinated. The success at getting past participants to pledge their time and money to the upcoming elections bodes well at helping the "flash campaign" become, if not permanent, more than just a flash in the pan.

Boyd and Blades had established that the Internet could be an effective means to create a large grassroots campaign almost instantly, and that, more importantly, it was possible to start it without the enormous resources. And they had tapped into a normally untapped resource for grassroots campaigns, non-activists. Later, other groups including the Libertarian Party would use the "Censure and Move On" campaign as a template for other campaigns: find a provocative message, use the Internet to reach large numbers of people, and make it easy for people to participate.

Chapter 4 Teaching an Old Medium New Tricks

Radio on Steroids

R adio is a survivor. It is the first broadcast
electronic mass medium, and unlike the
telegraph system, the radio has remained a
powerful and dynamic medium. In the early days,
people marveled at hearing disembodied voices from
afar, voices that traveled invisibly through the air,
through the walls of their houses, into their simple
crystal sets. Later, radio receivers grew larger, more
complex and more powerful with the advent of
vacuum tubes. Families gathered around their living
room sets to listen to President Franklin Roosevelt's
fireside chats, to Jack Benny's "feud" with fellow
comic Fred Allen, to the adventures of the Green
Hornet and the Lone Ranger—and to Arturo Toscanini
conducting the NBC Symphony Orchestra.

Then television appeared and challenged radio as a
broadcast medium. And as television sets became
more affordable, the importance of radio diminished.
But radio—now solid state and more powerful and
dramatically more compact than in the days of vacuum
tubes—survived by adapting to a new environment,
filling niches that other media couldn't. Before television everyone in a radio station's listening area (the
geographical range of a radio signal) was the intended
audience. Radio networks competed for an entire

population, much as the television networks do now. Unable to compete for the whole audience, since television supplanted radio as the basic family entertainment medium, radio stations were forced to try different ways to reach audiences.

Radio network stations had broadcast a mixed programming of soap operas, comedy shows, kids' shows, dramas, and live music. With television supplanting radio in delivering those types of programs, many radio stations began into broadcasting recorded music and focusing on different types of listeners. Today there are religious stations, news stations, stations for the young, stations for the old, country music stations, classical music stations, stations that serve minority communities, dividing the population into smaller and smaller audience segments. Rather than broadcasting to families gathered in their living rooms, radio now broadcasts to individuals jogging or driving in their cars and groups of coworkers in factories or offices. And radio—segmented and narrowly targeted—survived and prospered.

At first, the success of the Internet did not interfere with radio's success. Music and audio generally did not do well when transmitted over the Internet. As the Internet grew in popularity and connections allowed for greater bandwidth, a new radio format was born—Internet Radio—taking advantage of growing numbers of computers that had audio. RealNetworks pioneered the technology of streaming audio, a technology that allows audio files to be heard in real time. Internet radio currently has some major drawbacks: generally poor quality audio compared to radio, does not come installed in cars, and it is not easily portable.

Rather than working against radio, the development of Internet radio and the World Wide Web has helped extend the reach of local radio stations past the range of their radio waves. Broadcast radio stations may eventually face serious competition on the Internet from non-broadcast Internet-based stations. Or, perhaps the two will merge. At present, broadcast radio and the Internet are sibling media who complement each other.

Talk radio may be the best example of how the two media can bolster each other. In the broadcast medium, talk radio provides a strictly limited amount of audience interaction. There are, after all, only sixty minutes in an hour. Only a limited number of callers can be accommodated in one, two, or three hours, and those who get on the air are limited in how long they can talk, rant or rave. All those limits are off when the show goes on the Internet. Anyone can comment, and comments can be as long as the participant chooses. It's not the same thing as phoning in and actually speaking with the talk show host (or a guest expert or celebrity) before an audience of thousands. Callers find it exciting to be part of a discussion heard by the public.

By combining the popularity of talk radio, and its wild and colorful hosts and its limited number of callers with the greatly increased opportunity for interactive participation afforded to Web-based communication, Internet talk radio opens new vistas for the hybrid media mix. Some talk show hosts have begun to exploit these opportunities.

Radio Mayor of San Diego

Like radio, Roger Hedgecock is a survivor. Hedgecock had been elected mayor of San Diego in 1983, but he was forced to resign two years later after a jury convicted him of perjury and conspiracy in connection with the receipt of more than

$350,000 in illegal campaign contributions. Although he would later have his convictions overturned, he had already turned to talk radio for a new career. Much like Jerry Springer, a former Mayor and City Councilman in Cincinnati, Ohio, Hedgecock has bounced back from disaster to achieve larger success.

Perhaps Hedgecock might have battled his way back into elected politics, but he seems to feel more at home on the air. There is a smoothness and easy authority in his voice, and his views and opinions are now unfettered by the normal constraints of political life. Here he can promote what he believes are the good things in life, such as gun ownership, and rail against the demons: potholes, the IRS, and President Clinton. His daily three hour radio show is filled with discussions of local and national politics as he holds court and rules over San Diego from the airwaves.

Hedgecock is the number one radio show host in Southern California. The San Diego chapter of the National Organization for Women and others can complain about his comments on women, gays and immigrants, but the "radio mayor of San Diego" holds an office from which he can't be voted out.

While his politics may be reactionary, Hedgecock's sense of his medium is forward thinking. He has taken his radio format into new areas, integrating several novel features, including a Web site. In the middle 1990s, Hedgecock realized that the Internet offered several possibilities for extending the reach of his radio presence. He created a Web site to complement his on-air presence. His site is not a separate venture from his show; it is fully integrated into the radio program. The Web site and the broadcast rely on each other. Roger Hedgecock has strengthened his relationship with his audience through his Web site.

Each afternoon Hedgecock reaches out to a large, and mostly right wing, audience in Southern California, focusing their attention on conservative causes. Radio brings them in, but it is the Internet that permits them to become full fledged followers. Their energy feeds the show and Hedgecock skillfully directs that energy into political action.

One of Hedgecock's favorite targets is President Clinton and the President's policies. Like most conservative talk show hosts across the United States—and tabloid television hosts— the impeachment process offered a year-long focus on President Clinton's alleged wrongdoing.

More than a commentator, Hedgecock advocated the cause of impeachment, and he used his radio and Internet presence to move people to political action in support of impeachment. And Hedgecock knew his audience. Solid social conservatives, they were predisposed to trying to dispose of Clinton. The question was: Without some organization, would their voices go unheeded?

Of course, Hedgecock was not the first to use radio to rally an audience for a right wing cause. In the 1930s, Father Charles E. Coughlin had used radio to convey his emotional far right message to a national audience. But Hedgecock understood that it would take more than his voice discussing the issue on the radio to get Congress to impeach Clinton. And, because Hedgecock had more than just the airwaves at his disposal, he saw that he could sculpt and channel his audience into action with pioneering use of the Internet. Radio would carry the call to arms; the computer would be the arms.

For years, Hedgecock had posted the e-mail addresses of members of Congress, at least those that had them. As the time came closer to when the House of Representatives would vote on the impeachment, he wanted a better way to allow his audience to reach Congress. With the help of his son Chris Hedgecock, who has a Web design firm, he established a political action section allowing a listener to quickly and easily send a message to his own congressperson. An automated web service was fully integrated into the show's site, helping to funnel the pro-impeachment messages of thousands of Roger Hedgecock listeners to Congress.

In addition to the direct action, an entire community was created through the Web site. Hedgecock's radio show can hold the attention of listeners only for the duration of his program. His Internet site allows the listeners to become part of an activist network united by their interest in the mayor's radio show. This online community includes the listeners, host Roger Hedgecock, the staff of the radio show, and the radio show guests. But it also includes like-minded people's Web sites, as well as advertisers who are marketing to a self-selected segment of social conservative people.

The Hedgecock Web site included links to (and snippets of) other anti-Clinton material. Web site visitors could find myriad material, some of which could never be conveyed over the radio: sites with song lyrics, a child's perspective of Clinton as role model, the Starr report in all its detail, and satirical articles about the Clinton administration.

This material helps to shape the boundaries of the community. Viewers who are not comfortable with this material will stay away. Viewers who resonate with these materials will keep visiting the site.

Being a community means communicating with each other. Only a limited number of listeners can call and talk with Hedgecock on the radio show and have their comments heard by thousands of other listeners. Most of the mayor's fans can't be part of the on-air discussion. But everyone with a computer on the Internet can participate in the online discussion. This has the effect of multiplying the amount of time people spend relating to the show.

As the impeachment process progressed, discussion participants had made their views known in a very public way. They moved from being passive listeners to becoming activists for the cause. And the discussion group can encompass a much larger group than on-air callers.

Hedgecock's reach had the potential to extend beyond the large area to which the radio towers broadcast his show, going out to anyone, anywhere with a computer that has audio and is connected to the Internet. The Internet version of his show is available either by going to his Web site or to *Broadcast.com*, a Web site that carries a variety of radio and TV programs. Nonetheless, Hedgecock's audience is still largely a local audience, residing in the San Diego area.

While the Web site virtually carried the voices of this community to Washington, a Hedgecock-led "Hold Their Feet to the Fire" trip carried community members quite literally across the continent to the nation's capital. They brought the radio show with them; Hedgecock broadcast from Washington all week. The trip information was included on the Web site. Listeners who couldn't come along could follow the trip from the text and pictures on the site.

Participants in the "Hold Their Feet to the Fire" trip also had the chance to visit Washington, D.C., guided by their favorite on-air personality. And they were warmly received in San Diego Republican Congressman Jim Rogan's office.

With the merger of talk radio and the Net, Hedgecock stretched the role of talk show host to give himself a bigger platform than if he had never lost the mayoralty. And he fundamentally changed what radio is and can be. Unlike the "Censure and Move On" campaign, which focused on finding people to participate in political action, Hedgecock has concentrated on helping his current audience take political action. His audience is now a political entity which he can help lead into battle, fighting for the causes that they collectively believe in, from impeaching a president to fixing potholes.

Tortoise Beats the Hares

"Post the story to the Web site!" may not have the same dramatic ring to it as "Stop the presses!" But as the delivery of information closes in on the speed of thought, nothing can beat the dramatic speed of the Internet. And that's how *Roll Call* (one of Capitol Hill's two newspapers) was able to break one of its biggest stories of the year. Congressman Robert Livingston (R-LA), chosen Speaker-designate by the Republican Congress, had been found to have had an extramarital affair. *Roll Call* is published in newspaper form only twice a week. And the story was too hot to hold for the next printing of the paper.

Roll Call is much like a small town paper. Its readership is concentrated on Capitol Hill. Each congressional office receives several copies that immediately get distributed and read. Unlike the national news media that churn out stories that originate in Congress, *Roll Call* often focuses on the institution itself.

Sports coverage consists of the results of the annual baseball game between Democratic and Republican members of Congress. Readers often find that news items are about the Congressional office that employs them, or one of the other offices in their corridor. And although many of the stories it carries have national implications, those stories are just local news on Capitol Hill. Few know Capitol Hill better than *Roll Call*.

It had been a tumultuous year, with big messy stories littering the way, starting with the Drudge Report breaking the Monica Lewinsky story. Matt Drudge had scooped everyone, posting the story on his news site. There was a time not long ago when stories like these would never have been published. Now, after the rise of tabloid TV, after Drudge, and after Ken Starr, sexual peccadilloes had become the meat of American journalism. After the Starr report was made public, it was clear that no story was out of bounds. Somehow, what used to be the sewage system now flowed into the mainstream, and political reporting now meant catching stories before they fell into the tidal basin.

Salon, a magazine published through the Internet, ran a story about Chairman Henry Hyde, (R-IL) and an extramarital affair. The story on Hyde quickly gained national attention. It seemed to be the beginning of a tit for tat war between Clinton haters and Clinton supporters. The story of infidelity was intended to show the hypocrisy of those that were peering into the private life of Clinton. And various news outlets hung around waiting to fish out similar new stories.

The 1998 congressional election had gone badly for the
Republicans, and Speaker Newt Gingrich received much of
the blame. The Clinton impeachment had not helped convince
the voters to turn out against loyal Democrats in Congress.
And the Republican leadership had not found any other
causes to support the usual gains that the Presidents' opposition makes in congressional seats in mid-term elections.
Speaker Gingrich ducked out of what was likely to be an
embarrassing loss for a new term as speaker even as he was
reelected by a wide margin as the representative for his
congressional district.

To avoid further appearances of weakness the Republicans
quickly pushed forward Congressman Bob Livingston as a
candidate with substantial credentials for speaker. As Chairman of the Appropriations Committee, Livingston was one of
the most powerful people in Washington. He quickly garnered
nearly unanimous support in the Republican Conference. But
in the highly charged atmosphere and with all bets off on
exposing personal indiscretions, any prominent politician
would be subject to extra scrutiny. Especially if he was about
to become speaker of a House that was calling on the Senate
to oust the president. And someone had dished the dirt on
Livingston.

Jim VandeHei, a reporter for *Roll Call*, had stalked Livingston
for a quote on the allegation. He approached Livingston, who
was coming out of a closed meeting at around 5:30 PM, for a
comment. And Livingston gave him, not only a comment on
the allegations, but confirmation that it was true. And then the
clock began ticking. Other reporters had seen the interchange
between the Speaker-designee Livingston and Jim VandeHei,
and realized that *Roll Call* had the story and they were hot on
his trail.

As the last pieces were falling into place, *Roll Call* needed a way to run the story while it was still an exclusive. Minutes, even seconds, counted. It would have been impossible to go to press to print out a special edition. But breaking a big story is the adrenaline that drives reporters to heroic feats. And *Roll Call* could only break the story by publishing to its Web site edition. In a well coordinated effort between Mitchelle Stephenson of *Roll Call* and Kevin Rooney who maintained the Web site, the story was electronically transferred to the *Roll Call* Web site.

Mitchelle Stephenson, instead of shouting above the roar of the presses to get the story out, needed only speak on the phone with Kevin Rooney who was only a few clicks away from changing the Web site. And it was but a half an hour after the confirmation of the story that the article was electronically sent to Rooney, who then posted it to the *Roll Call* Web site.

Within seconds of posting the story on Livingston, *Roll Call* announced their news scoop in a dramatic television announcement. Morton Kondracke, the Executive Editor of *Roll Call* and well known political commentator, was to appear on Fox Television news show hosted by Brit Hume. Just before Kondracke came on the program he was alerted that the story had been published, on the *Roll Call* Web site. And then, on the air, he announced the big story. *Roll Call* had scooped the rest.

As the story spread, other journalists referred to the story as "the *Roll Call* story" on Livingston's marital infidelity. Millions of people learned of the story by watching it on the evening news. *Roll Call's* site was the evidence that *Roll Call* had the story first. And it was that Web page that millions saw, but mainly as a graphic for the TV news shows. The site itself was very difficult to get through to because Internet traffic over-loaded the server.

Its Capitol Hill readership mainly feels *Roll Call's* presence by its distribution in paper form. The paper is still very popular and an important addition to the reception area of many offices in the Capitol. The Web, as an alternative means of publishing, provided *Roll Call* with the opportunity to shine as a fast moving operation, despite its normal biweekly news cycle, a pace that suits the type of news this small town paper normally reports.

In a speech from the floor of Congress Livingston called on the President to resign. And then, with no warning, Livingston announced his own resignation from Congress. From being pressed for confirmation of the rumor, he had seen the writing on the wall, or more accurately the text on the Web.

Web to the Mother Ship

The big news organizations have taken the Internet very seriously. With a huge potential online audience, they cannot afford to dismiss the Internet. Most news organizations have created an online presence to be an extension of their main outlet, whether television or newspaper. And they have a huge advantage over new Internet-based competition, loads of content ready to post to the Web and a steady revenue stream from their other outlets.

Lisa Todorovich, staff member on *The Washington Post* Web-site, described the print version of *The Washington Post* as the "mother ship publication." Newspapers such as the *San Francisco Chronicle*, the *New York Times*, the *Wall Street*

Journal, and the Peoria *Journal Star;* television networks including ABC, NBC, CBS, and Fox; magazines including *Time, Newsweek,* and *The Nation* all have Web sites. It feels almost natural that all publications and public and private organizations have Web addresses: *.com, .org, .gov,* and *.edu* have become as easily recognizable organizational identifiers as inc. and co. Media sites live in symbiotic relationships with their "mother ships," not as replacement vessels.

Computer displays cannot mimic the tactile sensations of holding a newspaper in your hands. The paper version is easily portable, can be stretched out, can be folded, can be read while standing in a crowded bus or subway car, can be clipped and filed and has many other qualities that Internet technology lacks. *The Washington Post* can be delivered to homes throughout the capital area, and it can be found at news stands and vending machines; offering a near total saturation of an area. Although increasing quickly, the potential readership of the Internet version in the same area is substantially lower.

On the other hand, newsprint cannot easily mimic the Internet's ability to allow the reader to customize the experience, to extend content that will not fit in the limited space of the old medium, and to include varied media formats. The Internet version makes *The Washington Post* a more versatile news outlet.

Choosing to create a site on the Internet reflects a realization that the Internet is a powerful medium that can be a mirror to everything that exists in the printed world. The Internet provides increased readership without the cost of additional newsprint. And it gives the publishers the ability to post *The Washington Post* instantaneously throughout the world.

The Washington Post Company owns several news outlets besides the flagship newspaper: newspapers in other cities, magazines, television stations, and cable television systems. But unlike previous electronic ventures, the Web site has the same name as the newspaper and is tightly integrated in terms of content. (And many of *The Washington Post* Company's other ventures have corresponding Web sites.)

Branding, the use of naming products so they can be easily recognized allows a company to create an aura about their products. *The Washington Post* has leveraged the use of its name to create instant recognition of its Web site and make it clear that it will use the same journalistic traits in its site as in its paper version. Readers who have come to appreciate the newspaper will assume that the Web site carries on the same tradition.

But the association between the two media is more than by name and by content. The two enhance each other's capabilities. For example, the 1998 election returns were processed by the Web site staff as received from the Associated Press. Then the print reporters were able to base their stories on the posted results. And the Starr report was first received by the Web staff, then checked by the print staff, then posted by the Web staff, and then used for the print version. *The Washington Post* newspaper is being changed by association with its Web site, often giving it an edge much like the edge *Roll Call* enjoyed in releasing the story about Congressman Livingston.

As the potential readership has drastically increased by publishing to the Web, so has the number of competitors. In Washington, D.C., there is only one major competing local daily newspaper, *The Washington Times*, and only a few other papers that are generally available to the public. On the Web, the competition is nearly infinite. Among the main sources of competition are other news outlets that are already established off the Web: ABC, CNN, MSNBC, and almost every other newspaper in the country. And each brings with it a unique flavor, from the fast paced, always-on news cycle of CNN to that "old gray lady," the *New York Times*. On the Web, all of these news outlets have an even playing field, access to the same audience, the ability to match the technology of competitors, and the ability to overcome the restrictions of their original media.

And *The Washington Post* uses Internet technology that allows readers to easily send messages to their member of Congress. By providing this capability, it has given its readers the ability to move from merely reading the news to directly influencing it. *The Washington Post*, like Roger Hedgecock and his radio show, is helping its audience to take political action, albeit in a more neutral way.

Just as radio programming changed because of what was going on in other media, news organizations are quickly adapting to the new landscape. And those changes are, in turn, changing how political discourse takes place. From providing a more dynamic medium to creating a means for the audience to participate politically, large news organizations that have included an Internet outlet are now much stronger and likely to keep and extend their audiences.

Chapter 5

Meet the Cyber-
entrepreneurs

The Internet has been described as a truly
democratic medium, a forum for the free flow
of information and ideas. In this environment,
citizens and their representatives—freed from the
high costs of traditional political participation—can
communicate more openly, with little regard to
expense or the will of media gatekeepers. And while
this principle of "free" and "open" access is alive and
well in cyberspace, the fact remains: some of the most
significant tools for advancing our democracy online
have been developed by cyberentrepreneurs, people
with good ideas and a profit motive.

Doug Bailey, Phil Noble, Bob Hansan, Mark West,
Kevin Rooney, and Kathleen deLaski are among those
entrepreneurs and corporate pioneers who have made
a significant contribution to democracy online. They
are important players who are developing products—
for a profit—that support citizen interaction with
government and voter interaction with candidates.

Doug Bailey

Doug Bailey is a visionary whose early electronic
media successes helped create online political
journalism. He has also nurtured a crop of young

political and media experts who are themselves helping to pioneer the political use of the Internet

Bailey was an established Republican consultant who came out of the moderate Nelson Rockefeller wing of the Party. In 1987, he stopped consulting and founded *The Hotline*, a highly successful annotated daily political news clipping and digest service that was originally delivered by fax, then later by electronic download via modem, and eventually posted to the Web. Bailey used new technology, which he describes as "covering the coverage." The extraordinary success of *The Hotline* —within the Beltway and political media circles— depends on the content. But it was the novel and timely method of delivery that allowed it to be so useful to its subscribers.

After selling *The Hotline* to *National Journal*, Bailey helped its new owners create another new vehicle for political news. Although he has periodically explored the feasibility of a politics channel on television, he decided to use the emerging technology of the World Wide Web to produce a new type of political journal. The Web was an inexpensive method to publish information, much cheaper than the start up costs involved in television production.

The new site was called *PoliticsUSA* and it was the first of its kind. Bailey and *National Journal* were able to create a site that, like *The Hotline* before it, brought coverage of politics into the arena of the immediate through its delivery method. The site later merged to become *PoliticsNow*. It was well regarded, winning critical acclaim from several Best-of-Web editorials; but after the 1996 election, its high-power partners (*National Journal*, *The Washington Post*, and ABC) disagreed on the course to follow and ended the experiment.

During the short life of *PoliticsUSA* and *PoliticsNow*, Bailey helped several writers get their first taste of Internet journalism, a taste that taught them the possibilities of using the Internet. Among Bailey's protégés are: Troy Schneider, now Editor of *National Journal's* commercially successful *Cloakroom.com*, the home of their many cover-the-coverage publications; Chuck Todd, now the widely respected political Editor of *The Hotline*; and Laura Dove and Lisa Todorovich, two journalists who would later play a role in turning the tables on the old media and demonstrating the power of the new.

The never-stop Bailey will use the 2000 elections to launch still another first—bringing video-on-demand to politics—through a creative exploitation of broadband technology. His *FreedomChannel.com* will allow users to "...dial up the candidates they want to hear from, on the issues they want to hear about, all at times of their choosing."

Phil Noble

Phil Noble was hooked on politics by the time he was nine years old. He campaigned for John Kennedy, doing literature drops for the candidate in South Carolina. Nearly 40 years and 250 political campaigns later, Noble is still at it. But these days, he's as likely to be campaigning in cyberspace as on the ground.

Noble, 48, tops the short list of political consultants who are using the Internet to advance politics. Through a series of "firsts"—both online and off—he has established himself as one of the players who are revolutionizing how voters, political consultants, and politicians use the Internet.

Noble, a one-time U.S. Senate policy analyst, understands the value of information and the significance of the Information Age. He began his political consulting business in 1979 as an opposition researcher. His job was to dig through public records in order to find damning evidence about his client's opponents. Over the years that followed, Noble's experience and reputation grew. Phil Noble & Associates consulted with hundreds of candidates and their campaigns for the White House, the U.S. House and Senate, foreign candidates and political parties in 33 countries.

A former defensive end on his college football team, Noble understands that being first is directly related to being fast. That's why, in 1994, before his competitors had even thought to post a Web site, Noble launched an Internet and New Technology arm to his firm. By 1996, the division had grown into its own enterprise. He called it PoliticsOnline.

Today, PoliticsOnline transforms Noble's ideas and predictions into salable products and services that make it easy for political professionals to use the Internet for politics. It's a simple enough concept, but the thinking that has gone into PoliticsOnline and the products Noble has delivered are definitely outside the box.

Noble and his firm wrote the first guide to politics and the Internet with *Campaigns & Elections* magazine, a booklet that explained—in layperson's terms—the relevance of the Net to politics and advocacy. He developed the first CD-ROM for candidates, designed to help campaigns integrate the Internet into their overall strategy. It provided useful information—everything from how to get Internet access to tips for building a Web site. It provided tools—from e-mail to fund raising—and techniques for using the Internet with the media, conducting research, building a base of volunteers and more.

In 1998, Noble released the first online campaign fund raising tool. It enabled voters to make guaranteed, secure online contributions to candidates—via the campaign Web site—in a matter of minutes, with the click of a mouse. It was quick and easy—five steps to contribute—and it didn't cost campaigns a cent to use. If campaigns generated contributions online, Noble simply took a percentage.

Perhaps more important than his line of Internet political products, Noble has become a spokesman for the cause of Internet democracy. He talks up cyberpolitics at events nationally and internationally and promotes—often to less technologically savvy political consultants—the importance of thinking about the medium as a tool for politics and advocacy. His expertise is in demand, particularly overseas, where foreign candidates increasingly seek out his services and his cybervision to promote their ideas and campaigns. And it's working: Noble touts an 85 percent winning record for his international campaigns.

When his colleagues express doubt about the potential of cyberspace to reinvigorate democracy, Noble talks to them in terms the naysayers can understand: he bets them steak dinners that cyberpolitics is for real. And, he hasn't had to pick up the tab yet.

To keep his colleagues and the public focused on the future of Internet democracy, he maintains a free Web site, *www.politicsonline.com.* It is updated daily with useful information and analysis of the Internet's political side and the campaigns using the Internet for politics. Recently, Noble added the "Politicker" to his list of accomplishments, a free e-mail journal that tracks the top cyberpolitical stories across the country. Each week, he delivers the Politicker to the desktop of more than 10,000 subscribers. He claims it is the world's largest political-insider e-mail list.

Throughout his career, Noble has made predictions that turned the heads of his political industry colleagues. Among his favorites, "The Internet is going to have a far greater impact in our lives than TV has." On this point—and so many others related to Internet politics—Noble is right.

Robert Hansan

At 35, Bob Hansan is the President and driving force behind Capitol Advantage, the nation's largest publisher of congressional directories and a pioneer in cyberadvocacy. Launched in 1986 with pooled resources and basement office space donated by his parents, Capitol Advantage has emerged as the global leader and innovator in developing Internet tools and services that promote dialogue and empower the user. Four top Web sites, including America Online, Microsoft, *USA Today Online*, and Yahoo use Capitol Advantage services and allow millions of people to become better informed about the political process and how to engage in grassroots activities.

First and foremost, Hansan is a businessman. He happens to like politics—and the notion of empowering citizens—but that isn't the reason the poli-sci major went into the business. He needed a job after college. And, he got one: President and CEO of Capitol Advantage, a company of one.

On the way to earning his own paycheck, Hansan staked out a living, built a successful congressional directory publishing business, and discovered a niche in cyberspace. Call it cyberadvocacy.

Hansan is the first to admit he didn't run to the Internet revolution with open arms. Like a lot of people, he was skeptical. He questioned the reliability of the technology and the viability of the Internet as a venue for profitable business. Over time, he became convinced that the cost of doing nothing was greater than the risk of doing something. If citizens could access congressional data online, free of charge, he surmised, the Internet had the potential to seriously undermine his existing directory business. And by this time, Hansan's congressional directory sales had grown into a $2 million-per-year enterprise.

The answer, he believed, was to build a congressional directory product line for the Web—marketed at a cost any association, nonprofit, corporation, or media company could afford—and through the organization's Web site accessible to every user, free of charge.

Mark West

Hansan hired Mark West, online manager for C-SPAN (Cable-Satellite Public Affairs Network) to help him create an online directory for Capitol Advantage. West, a 13 year veteran of the cable industries' nonprofit public affairs network, was politically aware and a cyberpioneer in his own rite. He conceived and managed C-SPAN's state-of-the-art Web site, designing the organization's online congressional directory and delivering live gavel-to-gavel audio coverage of Congress to the desktop of C-SPAN's online audience.

Hansan gave West the reins to build the new product and hire and manage the staff that would move the off-line directory business into the Digital Age. They called the online directory product, CapitolWiz . It used the existing congressional data— and stretched it to meet the opportunities of a new medium. In its first year out of development, 50 clients subscribed to receive the Web-based service. For $1,500, organizations could add 2,500 pages of legislative and government information to their Web sites. The service provided: bios, photos, and contact information for members of Congress and their staff; links to Thomas; tips on writing Congress; the capacity to post voting records and legislative alerts; and to highlight and monitor bills of interest to the client. And something new: the ability for Web surfers to interact with the directory. By entering their ZIP code, users could automatically identify their representative and senators, and, if they chose, e-mail or fax them —on the spot.

Clients simply linked to Capitol Advantage's server. West created a unique interface for each client that matched the look and feel of their own Web sites. From the standpoint of the Web user, the "XYZ" association provided valuable legislative content and a tool for constituent e-mail communication on their Web site. From the standpoint of the XYZ association, a small investment in CapitolWiz added functionality and important government affairs content to their site—without putting additional demands on their server or their staff.

Today, hundreds of clients use CapitolWiz and other online products developed by Capitol Advantage. The business is profitable—in fact, Internet sales now rival the traditional directory publishing business. And West has expanded Capitol Advantage's Web based product lines—down to the state legislative level and in totally new directions—to meet growing customer demand.

In the 12 years since the company first entered the marketplace, the goal has remained the same: to make a profit by providing information that enables citizens to enter in and impact the political process. And whether it has been Hansan's pocket sized printed directories or West's cyberbased legislative action tools, the company has found a way to deliver on this mission.

What makes Hansan and West relevant to a discussion of cyberadvocacy is the tools they've put into the hands of ordinary citizens. Before the online product was developed, before clients like America Online and American Association of Retired Persons made online congressional information available via their Web sites, most citizens didn't have easy access to congressional data. A small percentage may have had a printed congressional directory produced by the company, a competitor, or provided by an association or business. A Web-savvy constituent could visit C-SPAN's or the U.S. House Web site, download a lengthy list of representatives and their e-mail addresses, and try to figure out which one was their elected leader. But, it wasn't a powerful recipe for fostering greater citizen involvement.

Hansan and West developed a product that put people back in touch with the process, without making them feel sheepish for what they didn't know. The online directory product took the guesswork out of the process. If a user knew his ZIP code, he had enough information to identify his members of Congress—and to e-mail or fax them online. The product simplified the task of communicating with Congress and this, more than anything else, enabled more citizens to rejoin the political debate.

Citizens weren't the only ones empowered by the new tools. Suddenly, nontechnical types running the lobbying and government relations arms of the major organizations in town could use the Internet for advocacy. They didn't need to hire a Webmaster or learn HTML. They simply launched their Web browser, and entered a unique Web address and password issued to them by the company. From this password-protected administrative site on the company's server, clients could maintain and customize key aspects of the content that appeared on their own site using standard English. As easily as typing an e-mail message to a friend, they could post action alerts with ready made, flashing graphics, identify and post key votes on legislation, monitor sponsorship of bills, and more. The site looked professional—and so did the political staffer running it.

It was a powerful combination. And it helped to move a lot of e-mail onto Capitol Hill—two million messages in a seven month period. Hansan and West had discovered something important: grassroots activists hadn't thrown in the towel, they'd thrown away their typewriters and traded up for something better. They became cyberadvocates.

Kevin Rooney

Kevin Rooney's eyes were affixed on the computer monitor in his office in Capitol Advantage headquarters. His fingers hammered at the keyboard. It was after hours, and he was on the most serious of deadlines. The receptionist called into him from across the hall—there was an urgent phone call from his client at *Roll Call*. "Mort's going before the cameras in five minutes. Can you get it online?" the client asked Rooney. Of course he would, he had to.

Rooney hung up the phone. His palms were sweating. He had five minutes to post the story of the year to *Roll Call Online* before *Roll Call's* veteran newsman, Morton Kondracke, went live before the cameras. Kondracke's announcement would bring down U.S. Representative Bob Livingston (R-LA) and end his bid for Speaker of the House.

Rooney made the deadline with seconds to spare. Kondracke broke the story on Fox news. And *Roll Call Online*—the official Web site of the Capitol Hill newspaper—published the story first, scooping every press operation in town. At 7:00 p.m., just minutes after posting the story to the Web site, Rooney and Bob Hansan watched Tom Brokaw deliver the NBC Nightly News. He reported on the story of Livingston's extramarital affair. Positioned behind Brokaw's anchor desk was a computer—a visual for the viewing audience—displaying *Roll Call Online*, the turtle who beat the hare.

Rooney wasn't a reporter. He was an independent contractor on assignment as *Roll Call's* Web master, a thirty-something stockbroker-turned-Web-developer-entrepreneur who likes politics—and loves breaking new ground on the Internet. This time, breaking new ground meant helping *Roll Call* scoop Brokaw. It was all in a day's work—and it reflected the skills and attitude Hansan and Capitol Advantage had been looking for in staff.

Rooney actually posted what would become his own job to *Roll Call's* Web site—a Capitol Advantage "help wanted" ad for a Product Development Manager. When Hansan offered him the position, Rooney had one condition for his new employer: he would take the job, if he could continue to work with *Roll Call*. Hansan agreed—and the two set out to shake up the political side of the Internet.

Rooney has emerged as one of the leading developers of Internet democracy tools. Among his accomplishments: helping to create ElectionWiz, a service that connected voters—for the first time and in one place—to relevant online information for congressional races in their own district and gubernatorial races in their state. Says Rooney, " There was nothing like it out there. It has the potential to impact the political process like nothing else anybody has ever done."

Before Rooney developed ElectionWiz, politically engaged Web users had to hunt and peck to find voter information on the Internet. In the 1996 election year candidate sites were tough to find: first, because there weren't many candidates online; and second, because there wasn't a consistent scheme for naming campaign Web sites. There were a few "comprehensive" campaign sites that offered voters a collection of candidate information, but none provided the tools for voters to identify the candidates running for office in their own congressional district or state. Unless voters knew the candidates and/or their congressional district, the Web wasn't particularly helpful for gathering voter information.

The Web-based service envisioned by Rooney gave voters the ability to visit a Web site, type in their ZIP code, and immediately identify the congressional candidates running for office in their district and the gubernatorial candidates in the state. Voters could link to candidates' Web sites, voter registration information for their state, and campaign contribution reports. They could e-mail the candidates—asking questions about the issues or volunteering for their campaigns.

Rooney, a young and savvy entrepreneur, quietly contributed to a major improvement in the conduct of politics in cyberspace. The spin doctors were quick to say 1998 wasn't the Year of Internet Campaigning. But those who watched people like Rooney and tools like ElectionWiz knew the 1998 election cycle was definitely the start of something big. Big for Capitol Advantage, in terms of clients: America Online, the top Internet Service Provider, and *Washingtonpost.com*, a top five national news site, became the first to buy the new service. Big for Rooney and the staff, in terms of expectations: The development team spent months making sure they "got it right," ensuring that the interface was easy for voters to use and for their clients to administer the service's custom features. And, big for online campaigning: America Online's Election Section received 15 million page views during the 1998 election season. And, a study conducted by GOPAC and Hockaday Donatelli Campaign Solutions found that over half of those page views were due to the electronic ZIP code directory, ElectionWiz.

If there had been such a thing, Rooney would have made the list of the Internet's Most Valuable Players for the 1998 election season. And at America Online's Dulles, Virginia office, he would have had company.

Kathleen deLaski

Creative Center I at America Online (AOL) is actually a converted airplane hanger near Washington Dulles International airport. It's modern and industrial and filled to the rafters with staff, computers, and fast moving ideas for transforming the company—and the Internet. Kathleen deLaski, AOL's director of legislative and political programming, works there. Her charge: to navigate AOL's course to engage citizens in democracy.

deLaski is one of a handful of people whose day-to-day work significantly advances the Internet as a tool for citizen involvement. She is piloting uncharted terrain—fulfilling the profit making goals of a corporate enterprise while realizing the democratic vision of AOL's Chief Executive Officer, Steve Case. deLaski's contributions have increased AOL's subscriber base and reconnected ordinary people to their government and the electoral process.

Considering AOL's vast resources and reach, some might discount these successes as something less than a major feat. But when deLaski joined AOL in late 1995, it wasn't the online media hub we know today. The company had just 3 million subscribers. deLaski called it an "upstart kind of place." Moving AOL from upstart to multi-billion dollar Internet service and news machine was serious business. And she was an integral—and savvy—member of the in-flight crew.

deLaski describes her landing at AOL as a bit bumpy, a culture shock for a veteran television journalist. As a correspondent with ABC News' Washington Bureau, she had the inside track to cover politics and the Pentagon. She had served under President Clinton as his administration's Pentagon spokesperson, the first woman ever to fill the role. She commanded respect. She had access. And, she had credentials.

Her AOL assignment—to produce the service provider's first ever coverage of a political campaign—was something altogether different. It was definitely new and exciting. But "new and exciting" can be double edged swords, particularly in stodgy Washington. Inside-the-beltway politicos didn't know much about the Internet. And, to a large extent, they didn't care. deLaski and her online colleagues were treated by many as the unwelcome guests at a dinner party. This became abundantly clear at the 1996 party conventions.

In journalism and politics, the Democratic and Republican party conventions are among the premier events of the campaign season. Major network television reporters have the run of the house. They have "credentials," privileges to roam through the convention center. They have floor access to interview party officials and delegates, meet the candidates, and bring the convention story to a national television audience. During her years as a television journalist, deLaski never had a complaint about her spot on the convention seating chart. But, she did feel constrained by the medium itself—by the manner in which television limits reporting to nine second sound bites.

In 1996, everything changed. deLaski, now with AOL, would travel to the conventions as a member of the online media. She had the authority to decide exactly who, how, and what AOL's online site would cover. But she quickly discovered that online chat hosts faced a more basic dilemma: They weren't guaranteed a seat inside the Democratic or Republican party convention halls.

In 1996, the House and Senate press galleries served as the credentialing offices for the Democratic and Republican party conventions. The offices didn't simply give away credentials—especially to online media. They had to be convinced that AOL was for real.

It was a tough sell. When deLaski made her pitch, she couldn't demonstrate AOL's online site to the credentialing office

71

decision makers: The House and Senate galleries weren't exactly Internet-ready. Instead, she gave them paper printouts of AOL's online pages. In return, she received blank stares— but no credentials. She attempted to describe the live coverage AOL provided in its chat rooms. "Think of a talk show," she said, "think of "This Week with David Brinkley." She pointed to the pieces of paper. The staff pointed deLaski to the door.

deLaski is a journalist down to the core, and she wasn't about to give up so easily. She took her case directly to the Democratic and Republican parties. She told them it was in their best interest to credential AOL. Finally, they agreed. On the opening day of the Democratic convention, deLaski took her credentials to the Chicago stadium, home of the Chicago Bulls. Her former colleagues—the television reporters and crews—were stationed on the floor. The radio broadcasters were positioned in the midsection of bleachers on one end of the court. deLaski's seat, with the other online chat hosts, was strategically located in the top row of the bleachers—behind the stage.

deLaski couldn't see the proceedings from her seat in the Convention hall, but that didn't stop her from hosting chats and delivering political news to AOL's online audience. And, she was able to give her online audience something more: a taste of what it is to be a convention delegate. She invited delegates to submit daily journals of their experiences. Each day, they trekked their personal journals to the top bleacher, where deLaski posted their diaries to AOL's online site for viewing by subscribers across the country. Together, deLaski and her band of delegates helped AOL take one measurable step forward to reconnect people with politics.

deLaski took another virtual leap during the 1996 campaign season with the launch of "Head to Head." This area of the AOL site provided online comparisons of the 1996 presidential candidates, framed on the issues of concern to AOL subscribers. deLaski's product delivered exactly what subscribers wanted: no-frills, spin-free candidate information keyed to their concerns. AOL polled its audience to identify the top 10 priority issues and gave candidates the opportunity to submit—for posting to AOL's site—their position statements on each one.

Head to Head was a clear success with AOL's online audience. The traffic also revealed something important about cyberpolitics: voters valued Net offerings that cut through the spin and the clutter and helped them get the information they needed to make election day decisions. On election night 1996, AOL partnered with ABC to deliver live online election coverage. deLaski covered the chat room and special guests, including ABC anchor Peter Jennings, dropped in to provide AOL subscribers with breaking news coverage and chat with the participants. As the results would later show, Election 1996 was good for President Clinton. And, it was great for AOL and cyberpolitics.

Thanks to deLaski's vision and AOL's infrastructure, AOL received kudos for what it did—provide its online audience with strong election coverage—and for what it didn't—crash, despite healthy traffic to the site. The response, said deLaski, made her sit up and take notice, "We have a lot of people represented here. How do we harness that power to make the candidates pay attention so that they will address what AOL subscribers want the candidates to talk about?"

Since November 1996, deLaski has made it her dual mission to help AOL's online audience cut through the clutter and to encourage candidates to recognize and accept the power of the people's voice online. She got her next chance to deliver on this mission in the off year election of 1998.

deLaski knew that the biggest challenge in the off year was to help site visitors identify the candidates for key races. To meet this need, AOL signed on with Capitol Advantage to develop a customized version of its product, ElectionWiz. AOL site visitors simply typed in their ZIP code and received a list of the congressional and gubernatorial candidates running for office in their state and district. The product delivered on deLaski's promise: it connected citizens to useful voter information, including links to candidate Web sites and organized groups that maintain issue positions online. It gave AOL's audience an easy way to e-mail candidates for office. It provided tools and information—without the clutter.

In 1998, deLaski also continued to focus on activities that would strengthen the voice of AOL's members in the electoral process. AOL and the Alliance for Better Campaigns conducted a "national brainstorming" forum that enabled AOL subscribers to share their views and strategies for improving the conduct of political campaigns. AOL members were invited to rate the Alliance's proposed strategies—and to offer their own ideas—for strengthening campaigns and making politics more responsive. Among the pearls submitted by the 3,000-plus AOL subscriber participants: Candidates should be required to wear buttons that identify the names of their biggest contributors.

Traffic to AOL's election section proved deLaski right. AOL members loved "just the facts" journalism and access to quality information. They wanted to engage in a substantive dialogue on the issues. They needed and wanted to be heard. During the 1998 election season, the election section received 15 million page views—a 500 percent increase over 1996.

With the 1998 election now over, deLaski turned her attention to the final launch of "My Government." My Government utilized Hansan's CapitolWiz as a backbone, enabling AOL visitors to type in their ZIP code and identify and send e-mail to their members of Congress and state legislators. Using another provider, AOL connected site visitors to other useful information, telephone numbers, and, to the extent possible, e-mail addresses for state and local government offices, organizational agencies, and courts.

deLaski put these cyberpolitical tools to the test even before the official launch date of My Government. The weekend following the Starr report's release, AOL posted the cyber-lobbying capability to the site. In two days, deLaski and AOL delivered 160,000 e-mail to Congress. The onslaught of e-mail messages brought down Capitol Advantage's and Congress's servers. It was the kind of problem cyberpolitical types dream about. Capitol Advantage set up a separate server just to handle the AOL load. Today, My Government delivers up to 50,000 e-mail messages to the Hill weekly.

deLaski and AOL continue to promote civic activism by linking top news stories covered on the site to the My Government area of its service. Subscribers can read about the conditions in Kosovo and, then, with the click of their mouse, compose and send e-mail to their members of Congress on the issue. AOL's capability enhances the ability of ordinary citizens to localize national stories, to quickly determine their own elected leaders' views and votes and how those decisions impact on society. AOL subscribers are no longer passive observers. They have the tools to identify and learn about their elected leaders, to speak out to their representatives on issues as they are unfolding, and finally, to determine whether or not their congressional representatives support their stands on key legislation.

deLaski isn't resting on the success of My Government or Campaign '98. She has set her sites on the next election cycle and the next generation of news coverage. "What you saw in 1996 and even in 1998, there was the young Internet guru on every campaign, but he couldn't necessarily get the other people above him to pay attention."

At the time of this writing, in the early days of the 2000 election cycle, deLaski and AOL have already launched the site's election area. Preliminarily, the area tracks presidential candidates who have formally announced their intentions and links AOL subscribers to their official sites. AOL monitors presidential maybes—those individuals who have formed exploratory committees but who have not formally announced their candidacy. And, the site links to political news coverage from *National Journal, Intellectual Capital.com, New York Times*, and CBS News on AOL. Substantial additional coverage is planned for the site, including and expanding the offerings of 1998.

Today, it would be difficult for any lawmaker or candidate to ignore AOL's preeminence in connecting citizens with the tools to impact the political process. That, of course, is due to the commitment of deLaski and her superiors—and as deLaski is quick to point out—the vision of the man at the top, Steve Case.

Visionaries like Bailey, deLaski, Rooney, Hansan, West, and Noble are significantly strengthening the ability of ordinary citizens to influence the process. Together, they have developed and delivered cybertools directly to the public, turning heads and votes on Capitol Hill and likely very soon, the outcomes of elections. They have made it possible for voters to get informed, to get involved, and to commit dollars to campaigns from their desktop computers. They have helped to promote good citizenship and "free" and "open" access to our political process. And, these cyberentrepreneurs have achieved all this, while staking out a livelihood for themselves and the companies they represent.

Chapter 6 Case Studies

American Civil Liberties Union

"Call off your dogs," demanded the voice on
the phone. It was an urgent request made by the
district staff of a certain—now former—congresswoman to the headquarters office of the American
Civil Liberties Union (ACLU). The "dogs," as the staffer
referred to them, were actually active constituents
from the member's Pacific Northwest district. And,
they had just responded to an electronic whistle blown
by the ACLU: an e-mail action alert notifying them of
congressional action to "limit Americans' freedom of
expression."

Back at ACLU headquarters in Washington, D.C., a
staffer pushed a button at her computer keyboard. It
was a deceptively simple action that mobilized a
national network of cyberactivists, arming them with
the tools to learn about and respond to an issue
important to ACLU.

A few years before, it would have taken an entire
day—and the energies of every staff member and
intern at ACLU headquarters—to get the word out to
activists in the field. Now, one staff person could notify
upwards of 30,000 grassroots activists in minutes, with
little more than the click of a mouse. The message sent
out from the national office was accurate—up to the

minute—and it gave constituents on the ground everything they needed to speak out against a proposed constitutional amendment prohibiting desecration of the U.S. flag. From the e-mail message, constituents could immediately link to the ACLU's national Web site—and the online tools to identify their members of Congress and fax or e-mail their constituent message. This one alert helped to generate thousands of constituent e-mail and faxes to Congress. And, it clearly rattled at least one Congresswoman's staff.

The e-mail and faxes from ACLU supporters didn't reach Congress by chance. They were the end result of a well organized campaign and a firm commitment to online advocacy. Bob Kearney, ACLU's field director, made sure of that. When Kearney joined the organization in 1997, he convinced the ACLU to take a course of action—online action. He helped to "institutionalize" online advocacy as a legislative strategy—and it paid off.

ACLU now tops the short list of organizations that are effectively tapping the Internet's potential for political advocacy. They are cyberpioneers. And they're quickly disproving popularly held assumptions about average Americans' interest in politics and their willingness to engage in the political process.

ACLU's willingness to go where the activists are and to expend time and resources on a relatively new and unproven medium have positioned the organization at the front of the political pack, ahead of its friends and foes in the advocacy community.

It's All Organizing

Computer code aside, effective cyberorganizing and traditional grassroots organizing have a great deal in common. At the ACLU, Kearney and his colleagues daily leverage the online medium by applying what works for the organization off-line: "The fundamentals of what you do online," Kearney confirms, "are the same as what you do off-line. It's all organizing."

For each of the major issues confronting the organization in Congress, ACLU has devised an online strategy in concert with its field and lobbying programs. On the flag desecration amendment, for example, ACLU's Web site provided a synopsis of the flag desecration issue, fax and e-mail alert messages, talking points, and online action plans—including immediate opportunities for site visitors to e-mail or fax their legislators.

At last count, upwards of 20 issues were covered on the site, with topics ranging from cyberliberties to immigrant rights. And every e-mail and fax "action" by an activist on one of these issues generated still another opportunity—the chance to join ACLU's e-mail lobby list and receive e-mail alerts concerning pressing issues in Congress. ACLU Action, the grassroots lobbying list, now boasts a national subscriber base of more than 30,000 individuals, an activist list that most Washington advocacy groups—often still reliant on "pony express" outreach methods—would clearly envy. ACLU also maintains a media oriented list, "ACLU NewsFeed," and "ACLU Cyber-Liberties Update," a biweekly e-mail service that monitors rights and liberties online.

The Resource Connection

In cyberspace as in life, there's no such thing as a free lunch. Serious online organizing takes money, that is, if the goal is to "institutionalize" cyberadvocacy into an organization's overall operation. And, while e-mail is sometimes free, staffing, technology, training, consultants, advertising and promotion of a cyberadvocacy program require real money.

For the ACLU, says Kearney, the "dedication of resources clearly paid off." In the two years since the organization committed to online activism, its grassroots network has generated more than 148,000 constituent e-mail and faxes to Congress. And in the last year, the organization increased—by threefold—the size of its online lobbying e-mail list. With this grassroots cyberpower, ACLU was able to beat back an organized, multimillion dollar campaign to pass the proposed "flag desecration" amendment to the U.S. Constitution. The amendment won passage in the U.S. House of Representatives, but failed to garner sufficient support in the Senate to bring the issue up for floor consideration.

ACLU made a definitive resource commitment to cyberadvocacy—and targeted its dollars in the areas of staffing and technology. Kearney hired a full time cyberorganizer whose job it is to "mine the Net." The Internet organizer calls it the "coolest job title in the world." And, based on the results she has achieved, her employer must certainly agree.

Having a full time staff person committed to the project gives the organization an important edge. ACLU is able to communicate regularly with its growing activist base, keep legislative content on its site fresh and relevant, get the message out to other activist e-mail lists, bulletin boards, and Web sites, and conduct the kind of targeted issue-outreach that reaps rewards. "She gets out on the Internet, she drives traffic to the site," says Kearney. In addition, ACLU's online organizer maintains a database of "outlets" by issue—the groups, e-mail lists, and Web sites that have responded favorably to her posting. "The overall reaction has been extremely positive," she says. "Folks are eager to use the Net for what it was built for—getting information and making the connection."

Making the Connection and Getting Results Online

ACLU takes its online relationships seriously. Staff ensure the site content is up-to-date and identify on the site the revision dates of all the alerts, talking points, and summaries posted there. ACLU activists know that they can count on the organization to e-mail them whenever there is relevant news to report or action needed from the network.

ACLU's online organizer believes in "keeping it simple, not making folks work too hard to get active. And, once you have made contact with them, work to keep that relationship productive by not inundating them. Make sure that you maintain your credibility."

ACLU works hard to ensure that its site serves as a valuable resource for activism, committing dollars for Web-based technologies that make it easy to get and stay involved and to communicate with lawmakers on the organization's issues. The budget covers the costs of Web-based legislator-communication tools, including "free faxes" sent by ACLU activists from its Web site to members of Congress, and database management tools and software programs that help the online organizer do her job.

ACLU's commitment to cyberadvocacy is real and measurable. It can be counted—in dollars spent and staff hours allocated. Its results online are also easily measured; the Internet is a brutally accountable medium. How many e-mail were delivered? How many faxes transmitted? How many activists were added to the list? For better or worse, it is easy to measure success and failure online.

It's still possible for an organization to achieve overnight success on the Web with a "flash campaign" like "Censure and Move On" and without a significant resource commitment. But established, Web-savvy organizations—like the ACLU— wouldn't think of leaving their advocacy agendas to chance.

The March: Coming Together to Conquer Cancer

They came from all over the country—by bus, car, and plane—to the Mall in Washington, D.C. Giggling children. war veterans, politicians, celebrities, doctors and their patients, husbands and wives and survivors. They were 150,000 strong, and they had a message for Congress and President Clinton: It's time to get serious about curing cancer.

Organizers billed the event, "The March: Coming Together to Conquer Cancer." The 380-plus groups endorsing the March— including a broad array of cancer, health, patient, and professional medical organizations—had an ambitious goal. They wanted to put "cure," "cause," and "care" of cancer on the national political agenda. Their strategy: to deliver 100,000-plus people to the Mall on September 26, 1998 and to hold local events across the country.

It was a massive undertaking, the first and largest event of its kind. The coalition's chances for success hinged on its ability to organize, recruit and coordinate thousands of volunteers, add to the list of coalition partners, get the word out to potential supporters, and entice the press to cover the event. They needed to coordinate hundreds of details—from bus schedules to housing—and address logistical needs from volunteer-event matching to training.

The first decision was perhaps the toughest that any organization—or group of organizations—makes at the start of such an undertaking: whether and where to put the resources. The organizers hired a Web-savvy public affairs firm to design the overall organizing plan and a temporary staff to coordinate and manage the event. It was the right decision.

The planners recognized the importance of the Internet as a tool for grassroots organizing, and they integrated the Internet with more traditional organizing strategies to build a strong, on-the-ground campaign. The March may have been an off-line event, but it chartered new territory in cyberadvocacy. "We integrated the Internet as a tool to connect people, to help people find out how to get on a bus, to get details on the campaign," said Ken Deutsch, Vice President for Internet Strategic Communications with Issue Dynamics. "The Internet became a management tool and a new way to reach out and recruit people." It was also a powerful medium for communicating the campaign's message—one with the unique capacity to transform passive observers into activists.

The Message

The planners created a Web site for the event, and ensured that it delivered the message of the campaign. In as much as the message shaped the site, however, the Internet as a medium helped to shape—and expand—the message. Marshall McLuhan wrote: "It is the medium that shapes and controls the scale and form of human associations and

85

action." In the cybermedium, the coalition could quickly and powerfully carry its message to millions of people and transform those passive site visitors into activists.

The Web site gave visitors the ability to "experience" the message in ways not possible via other medium. Site visitors could see an instant calculation of cancer's human toll, an up-to-the-minute projection of the number of Americans diagnosed with cancer that year. They could establish an immediate relationship with the campaign by pledging to volunteer. They could read the personal stories of cancer survivors who were working to make a difference at the March. The site pushed the campaign's compelling and poignant message out to the public, and drew in potential activists to meet the organizing demands of the event.

E-Organizing

Every page of the Web site provided visitors at least one opportunity to volunteer. The options covered the gamut. Activists could pledge to attend the national event, register as a bus captain, even commit to organize a local or statewide March. Over 3,000 people volunteered directly from the site using a Web-based volunteer form.

The forms these activists completed became fodder for the organizers' database. As activists completed and submitted a volunteer form, the information was integrated directly with a database management system for the March, automating the process for updating and maintaining schedules, address lists, and more. Organizers connected to the database daily, enabling the system to route information requests and mail list updates and pledges to appropriate organization staff.

Organizers kept thousands of activists and the public-at-large informed and motivated about the event via a weekly e-mail newsletter disseminated by the campaign. The online format helped the coalition to cut down on mailing costs while strengthening the connection and relationship between the community and the event.

The Web site served as the organization's primary information source for the public. The site contained volunteer-training schedules, transportation and housing information, and a calendar of local events. The benefit to the campaign was measurable. Maintaining this information online helped to reduce the number of phone calls to the headquarters staff and put critical information at the fingertips of activists.

Coalition Building Online

Event organizers urged endorsers of the March to take part in two "e" activities: send e-mail recruitment messages to their own activist networks and post an online banner advertisement publicizing the March on their sites that linked to the coalition Web site. In September—the month of the March—338 Web sites had active links to the March site. One endorser, America Online, donated banner ads that delivered more than 7,000 distinct users to *www.themarch.org*.

E-Media

The Internet was an integrated element in the overall media strategy for the event. Free, public service announcement banner ads ran on major Web sites, including America Online and focus areas within I-Village. Paid banner ads also drove traffic to the site and potential activists to the site's online recruitment tools. Press releases, paid print advertisements, and e-mail updates all publicized the Web site address. And, the site was highlighted in free media coverage, including television, radio, and Internet stories.

The March demonstrated the effective role the Internet can play in building an online community of support to achieve an off-line objective. In the end, the Net helped the campaign deliver 150,000 people to the Mall, and manage events in every state and more than 200 community events scattered throughout the country. Most important, the use of the Net contributed to achievement of the larger goal: a 9 percent increase in the budget for the National Cancer Institute.

The coalition made a conscious decision to devote resources to cyberadvocacy. While the campaign wasn't an "Internet exclusive," it charted new territory by successfully integrating cybertools into the management and delivery of a national event. It was a wise use of the medium—and a high-yield investment.

You Can Bank on It

Once pioneers of cyberadvocacy had shown that the Internet is an effective tool, it was inevitable that various groups would try to copy the techniques and the success of those past efforts. And ease and speed of using the Internet allowed grassroots activism to be concentrated on new and previously unlikely targets. One of the most successful of these new cybercampaigns was waged against the FDIC (Federal Deposit Insurance Corporation), the federal agency that insures all depositors bank accounts to $100,000.

Every business day the federal government prints the *Federal Register*. Within its pages are the rules, proposed rules, and notices that federal agencies make public. When a federal agency posts a proposed rule, the public is often invited to comment. The agency will then consider the comments in the shaping of the rule. While most people have heard the phrase "write your Congressman," few people instinctively dream of trying to influence government workers who shape the nation's regulations. Congress is up for reelection regularly, but bureaucracy is forever.

The better regulations are written, the easier it will be for agencies to enforce them. And regulations are the means with which agencies implement the laws which Congress has passed, and Congress can always overrule the regulation with legislation. If comments from interested parties make sense and provide constructive criticism, agencies may take them into account in changing the proposed regulations.

The *Federal Register* has always been a daily printed document that is available through the Government Printing Office and certain libraries. More recently the *Federal Register* has been available electronically and now is free for access through the Internet. In addition to posting to the *Federal Register*, federal agencies often announce the proposed regulations by sending out press releases to the media. News of proposed regulations is covered by specialized media for the various regulated industries upon which the regulations can have a huge and direct impact. Some of the notices of proposed regulation include an e-mail address in addition to a postal address for comment.

Overall, the responses that are received come from organizations that have a direct interest in the area of regulation. The normal sources for comments received by federal agencies include law firms representing the affected industry and trade associations that often support the legislation that the regulations are based on. The comments become part of the official record and are made public.

In December 1998, four agencies with oversight of banks, the FDIC, The Board of Governors of the Federal Reserve System, the Office of the Comptroller of the Currency, and the Office of Thrift Supervision proposed the "Know Your Customer" regulations. The agencies proposed the regulation to help banks standardize policies used to identify and report possible criminal money laundering. Under the Bank Secrecy Act, banks are supposed to report suspicious activity to enforcement agencies. Already many banks had been adopting internal policies intended to help comply with the law. By having the FDIC create industry wide rules, all banks would be on a level playing field and also take the guesswork out of following the laws.

During the Great Depression, banks across the nation failed and depositors lost a great deal of their money. The FDIC was set up by the federal government to ensure that all depositors' accounts would be insured up to a certain level. And the FDIC was given power to regulate the banks to decrease the chance of failure and avoid the specter of massive bank failures ever happening again.

"Know Your Customer" means exactly that, banks should know who their customers are and be familiar with their banking. If bankers are familiar with their depositors, they should be able to identify those customers who deposit or transfer money gained through illegal means. Once having identified the illegal activity bankers would then have to report that activity to the proper authorities. And because all banks would abide by the same rules, it would make it difficult for criminals to find legitimate banks to launder their ill-gotten gains.

But the FDIC knew that there would be some controversy. To know your customer meant to know all your customers, and that means that banks would be in a position of investigating every customer. The FDIC alluded to the controversy in their press release: "This proposed "Know Your Customer" regulation has generated a great deal of public interest in advance of today's publication." But the FDIC and other agencies were not prepared for the tidal wave of opposition.

Not everybody is rushing to help law enforcement agencies catch criminals. The Libertarian Party stresses individual freedom in its public positions, often calling for rolling back laws that they feel restrict individual liberty. The Libertarian Party wants to avoid having government becoming more powerful and invasive of private lives. Their party platform takes a very strong stand on an individual's right to privacy.[1]

And in the context of the "Know Your Customer" regulations, the party felt the federal agencies were expanding their powers and unfairly infringing on privacy rights. They believed that the "Know Your Customer" regulations were pushing banks to spy on individuals and allowing law enforcement agencies easy access into personal affairs of ordinary citizens without reaching the Constitutional standard of probable cause. Banks are generally relied on to keep depositors' savings safe and are only concerned with the private details of customers when deciding on giving loans.

According to Steve Dasbach, the National Party Director of the Libertarian Party, they saw the second or third news notice regarding the proposed regulation in early January of 1999 in an Internet journal, *WorldNetDaily*. The party then

---

[1] Libertarian Party Platform. *www.lp.org/platform/pop.html*

moved to alert their membership and the public regarding the regulation and their opposition. This effort included sending out press releases to the media, including talk show hosts. They also had an e-mail list with approximately 10,000 people.

The Libertarian Party noticed that the story generated a great deal of notice. They believed it indicated there was enough opposition to show reason to make a campaign against the regulations. They saw indications that the privacy issue regarding the regulations would garner support from a wide cross-section of the country. The party had heard that the FDIC had already received a record breaking 10,000 messages, and the party felt they could help double the number through continued efforts. They decided to take advantage of the opportunity that FDIC created allowing messages sent by e-mail by setting up a more sophisticated campaign.

The Libertarian Party had already sent out e-mail notices in January 1999 to its membership list regarding the "Know Your Customer" regulations. They would need to try something more to make this a significant campaign. Steve Dasbach says that they looked around for ideas on how to organize a major campaign in a short amount of time, since there was less than two months before the FDIC stopped accepting comments. They were impressed with the success which the "Censure and Move On" campaign had with using the Internet and they set out to emulate that success by copying its methods.

The two most important methods copied were to create an issue specific Web site and an "e-mail your friends" campaign. The Web site would be the focus of the campaign and the Libertarian Party decided not to use their own Web site's name, but instead obtained a separate and easy to remember name for the campaign Web site, *www.defendyourprivacy.org.* The site was very straightforward, explaining the issue and providing an easy way to send a message to the FDIC. And the site linked to the FDIC, allowing anyone to see the actual proposed regulations.

The site became public on February 17, 1999, less than one month before the cutoff of comments. Although the number of messages that the FDIC had received was unprecedented, it had only been two months worth. The party ended up getting technology that also allowed the message to be copied to the individual's member of Congress and Senators. This was just a matter of checking on the ZIP code of the individual. In this way, the campaign simultaneously applied pressure on Congress which might eventually trump the regulations.

It was a successful gambit. The House of Representatives and the Senate ended up applying pressure on the FDIC.

And as more people participated and passed on the message to even more people, the press picked up on the growing success of the campaign and did stories that brought wider visibility to the site. Certain Web-based journals also encouraged participation by including a direct link to the campaign Web site as well as to the FDIC Web site.

The FDIC had been aware of possible negative reaction, but they could not have guessed the level of anger with which the public viewed the proposed regulation. And in a very open way the FDIC allowed the public a "real time" view to the number and type of public responses, since its site featured a table of the negative comments received. So throughout the campaign visitors to the FDIC site could see how the campaign was progressing. Respondents included banks, bank holding firms, law firms, associations, legislators and state regulators: numbering in total just over three thousand. These types of respondents could be expected for any comment opportunity for a regulatory agency. What was unusual was the number of individual respondents: over a quarter million. And over two-thirds of messages came directly through the Libertarian Party's Web site.

Also striking was the breakdown of reasons given for opposing the regulation. In every category of respondents, the leading reason given was privacy. Even the banks, which had received some pressure from customers, gave privacy as a greater concern than the cost of complying with the regulation. "Know Your Customer" became an orphan that no one wanted.

In the face of the opposition the FDIC officially gave notice that the proposed regulations were dead on arrival. In three short weeks the Libertarian Party had created the largest cybercampaign ever against a federal regulation.

The success of the campaign depended on several things coming together: a message that inflamed passions, the example of a successful campaign that could be evaluated, and inexpensive technology that could be quickly set up. In the case of commenting to a federal agency, only written comments are accepted. Only the Internet allows for low cost, nearly instant messaging. And the Libertarian Party proved that it was an effective tool.

The Save the E-Rate Campaign: A Personal Journal

This case study presents the personal experiences of author Pam Fielding, who designed and coordinated the 1998

*online advocacy campaign Web site for the Save the E-Rate
Coalition. Fielding and her colleagues—most notably
Carolyn Breedlove, Jon Bernstein, and Stephen Wollmer of
the National Education Association, and Michelle Richards
of the National School Boards Association—waged an online
battle, the first coalition campaign of its kind, to preserve
the federal program to wire America's schools and libraries
to the Internet.*

The Save the E-Rate Coalition represented six private and
public education groups: the National Education Association
(NEA), the National School Boards Association, the American
Association for School Administrators, the National Catholic
Educational Association, the U.S. Catholic Conference's
Department of Education, and the National Association of
Independent Schools. A splinter group of a larger coalition,
these were the few organizations willing to draw a line in the
sand against the telecommunications companies.

In the battle that was about to ensue, the opposing sides each
had a competitive advantage. The telecommunications
companies—AT&T, MCI, Sprint, BellSouth, GTE, and SBC
Communications—had lobbying power and deep pockets. The
associations had people power: thirty thousand teachers,
librarians, school board members, parents, and technology
staff connected by a cause—and electronic mail.

For more than two years, EdLiNC—the Education and
Libraries Network Coalition—negotiated in good faith with
Congress, the Federal Communications Commission (FCC),
the U.S. Department of Commerce, and the telecommunica-
tions companies to link schools and libraries to the Internet.
The deal was done.

Congress passed bipartisan legislation—the Telecommunications Act of 1996—allowing telephone, long-distance, and cable companies to compete against each other in the marketplace, creating new revenues, and dramatically lowering their costs to do business. In exchange, the companies agreed to use a tiny fraction of the profits they'd reap from the deal to help give schools and libraries affordable access to the Internet and other telecommunications services.

The plan—articulated in an amendment offered by Senators Olympia Snowe (R-ME), John Rockefeller (D-WV), J. James Exon (D-NE), and Robert Kerrey (D-NE)—would help break the digital divide for kids, schools, and libraries. The E-Rate provision was adopted with strong bipartisan support, thanks in large part to the leadership of the amendment's Senate authors, support from key members of the House of Representatives, including Representative Connie Morella (R-MD) and Commerce Committee Chairman Thomas Bliley (R-VA), and an unusual alliance of private and public education and library organizations that worked to secure its passage.

President Clinton signed the legislation and the Federal Communications Commission unanimously approved the rules that would guide the implementation of the E-Rate, or Education-Rate, program. A press conference heralded the huge win for consumers, children, and education.

More than 30,000 applications were received from public and private schools, libraries, school districts and educational and library agencies requesting the new E-Rate discounts. Applicants completed the required paperwork and extended promises to schoolchildren and library patrons. It was time for the telecommunications companies to ante-up the money that would fund the program.

The telecommunications companies' rumblings of opposition began on the same day the rules passed. It was too much money. The industry "couldn't afford" to pay. The long-distance carriers—AT&T and MCI—publicly suggested that costs might have to be passed onto consumers. Three local phone companies—BellSouth, GTE, and SBC Communications—filed a lawsuit on the E-Rate and the Universal Service program. Telecommunications lobbyists worked behind the scenes to pull the plug on the E-Rate program. Support for the program would soon fade along party lines.

May 6th marked the opening salvo of our campaign to save the E-Rate. From remote locations, six private and public education groups silently dispatched an urgent e-mail alert to tens of thousands of education supporters across the country. The message: Urge the FCC and Congress to save the E-Rate. The program to wire schools and libraries for the Internet is in jeopardy.

At NEA headquarters, my computer beeped—an audio notification of incoming e-mail to the Save the E-Rate Coalition. It was a fabulous sound and an affirmation that our little group had made the right decision.

Over the coming days, that Pentium would beep incessantly—two thousand times in twenty-four hours, twenty-two thousand times in just eight weeks. It was the battle cry of a wired army. The computer was rendered useless for anything else, but it didn't matter. Save the E-Rate supporters were fighting back.

From a desktop computer in El Paso, Texas, a teacher scanned our coalition alert and linked to the Save the E-Rate coalition Web site. Everything she needed was displayed on her screen: a run-down of the issue, links to the coalition partners, and the tools to identify and e-mail directly from the site her members of Congress, the FCC commissioners, and the CEOs of the telecommunications companies.

She entered her ZIP code. The names of her representative and senators appeared on the screen. She selected "all" to address the message to all three members, plus the FCC and the telecommunications heads. In the space provided, she entered her name and address. Her message could now be quickly identified as a constituent communication. She began to compose her message in the e-mail form.

"As a member of the teaching profession, a taxpayer, and a parent of a child in the public schools," she typed, "I feel that it is of the utmost importance that Congress fully support full funding and services for the E-Rate telecommunications discounts for schools and libraries. I work in one of the poorest school districts in Texas, San Elizario ISD in El Paso County. Without these E-Rates, my children in the classroom would not have the opportunity to become computer literate or surf the Information Highway."

It was the beginning of a wired revolution, launched in 48-hours with $1,200 and borrowed time from a few NEA and National School Boards Association staff.

Nine Thousand Messages

In the second week of the campaign, the coalition e-mailed the cybertroops with a second urgent appeal: nine thousand messages had been sent from the coalition Web site, but new threats had emerged. The fight to save the E-rate was far from over.

Rep. Thomas Bliley (R-VA) and Sen. John McCain (R-AZ), chairmen of the influential U.S. House and Senate Commerce committees, had called on the FCC to immediately suspend the E-Rate program. They wanted an impact study of the program's effect on customer phone bills. Other critics on the Hill introduced legislation to eliminate certain telecommunications services—including internal connections—from the list of services eligible for discounts. The impact on schools and libraries would be severe: according to the nonprofit entity established to administer the E-Rate program, more than half the money requested by schools and libraries would cover the costs to install wiring inside classrooms and libraries.

Time magazine published a devastating article by Karen Tumulty and John Tickerson entitled "Gore's Costly High-Wire Act." The reporters characterized congressional criticism of the E-Rate as an "out of control entitlement" and an example of cyberpolitics to support Gore's 2000 campaign. The article also contained an essay by David Gelerntner, a computer science professor from Yale, who suggested that the Internet would hurt—not help—kids in acquiring basic skills. This, despite a study by the U.S. Department of Education that found students in classes that use computers outperform their peers on standardized basic-skills tests by an average of thirty percent.

Responding to threats of telephone bill hikes, consumer groups joined in the fight. On May 21, the Consumers Union and the Consumer Federation of America sent a joint letter to the FCC, calling on the commission to suspend collection of E-Rate funds: The program should be shut down until the FCC addressed their concerns about increasing customer phone bills.

By now, our second e-mail message reached the desktops of our core activist group. Within hours, constituent e-mail counts climbed on Capitol Hill and on the Save the E-Rate coalition Web site. We watched the incoming e-mail. They were strong messages of support. And some of them provided evidence of a cyber ripple effect: community members, students, business people, and parents from outside our activist base were sending messages from the site. It became clear that our cybertroops were forwarding our message. They were speaking out and organizing their own communities—on and off-line—to save the E-Rate.

The E-Rate campaign received another boost in the form of a letter to the FCC, signed by Democratic and Republican senators—including Edward Kennedy (D-MA), Rick Santorum (R-PA), James Jeffords (R-VT), Christopher Dodd (D-CT), John D. (Jay) Rockefeller IV (D-WV), Robert Kerrey (D-NE), John Chafee (R-RI), and Olympia Snowe (R-ME). The Senators and three of the architects of the original E-Rate amendment—Rockefeller, Kerrey and Snowe—urged the commission to fully fund the E-Rate program.

The E-Rate Becomes An E-Story

On May 28, Save the E-Rate Coalition issued a press release with distinct cyberappeal. The fight to save the E-Rate for schools and libraries had now generated 10,000 e-mail messages to the FCC, Congress, and telecommunications companies. Coalition members issued their own releases and worked the story with national and regional press contacts. Even the firm whose technology powered the site issued a release highlighting the campaign's success.

The online campaign piqued the interests of the press: In time, the *New York Times* on the Web, *USA Today Online*, the *Philadelphia Inquirer, The Washington Times, Education Daily*, and *Education Week* had covered the campaign—linking to the site or carrying the site address on their printed pages. Rush Limbaugh, conservative talk radio show host, also covered the online campaign in his live radio address.

As press calls came into the coalition, the relative value of e-mail messages from E-Rate supporters grew exponentially. Not only were they a tool for communicating with Congress, the FCC, and the telecommunications companies, they were fodder for news stories. With messages in hand, we had a tool for "localizing" the issue with the press. They were the evidence that proposed E-Rate cuts would devastate individual schools and libraries. They were leads for the reporters who contacted us after the release was issued. In less than 24-hours, we were able to e-mail supporters and request the opportunity to release their e-mails to the press, and with approvals in hand, provide reporters with contact information to immediately reach teachers, librarians, business people, and parents on the E-Rate issue.

On the same day that the Save the E-Rate Coalition issued its release, AT&T made its own E-Rate announcement: the company confirmed it would begin charging customers to pay its costs for the E-Rate program and other aspects of universal service. Within days, MCI followed suit.

AT&T's announcement was a deal-killer, to be certain. And it belied certain facts. The charge to be posted on customer phone bills would pay for more than E-Rate service for schools and libraries. Approximately half of the AT&T charge would support basic phone service in rural areas and for low-income consumers—a component of universal service in place since 1934. Worse yet, AT&T had no plans to post on customer bills a line-item to reflect the dramatic reductions the carrier received in local access fees. FCC Chairman William Kennard wrote to the top long-distance companies, demanding proof that the carriers returned to consumers—not kept—profits from the reduced access charges it received as a result of the Telecommunications Act implementation.

With the E-Rate officially in turmoil, the FCC floated a plan to salvage the deal. First, in response to congressional and General Accounting Office concerns, the FCC would merge the nonprofit entity it established to administer the E-rate program, the Schools and Libraries Corporation, with another entity under its purview, the Universal Service Administrative Corporation. This would neutralize the charge it had erected a "bloated federal bureaucracy" to oversee the program. Second, the FCC proposed lowering the financial bar for the telecommunications companies by cutting the size of the E-Rate program for schools and libraries. The industry would need to bring only $1.67 billion to the table in 1998, rather than the $2.02 billion amount approved during the FCC rulemaking process. It was $350 million short of actual demand, but, the FCC contended, the plan might prevent phone rate increases for consumers. The FCC solicited public comment on the plan. And they got it, courtesy of Save the E-Rate Coalition supporters.

Messages poured into the coalition, one beep at a time. Printed copies of the e-mail now filled a metal, five-drawer filing cabinet, from top to bottom. They were also filling the e-mail boxes of our targets: Congress, the FCC, and the telecommunications companies.

"Take us off." That was the request made by a major phone company (and campaign target) to the firm hired to host our coalition Web site. It was a serious request—and in our view—a questionable tactic for a corporation that was purportedly interested in serving its customers. The message was relayed to the coalition for response, and we provided one: a polite "no."

But the company didn't take "no" for an answer. They simply pulled the plug on their e-mail. For the coalition, it was a stunning revelation. Our e-mail was getting noticed by a major telecommunications company. And we weren't about to call it quits. The campaign found another e-mail address for the carrier and posted it to the site.

The battle reached crisis proportions in early June. The June 2nd edition of *The Washington Post* carried an opinion piece by James Glassman, entitled "Gore's Internet Fiasco." The op-ed charged that the E-Rate program was "Al Gore's pet project," that the benefits of linking children to the Internet are "uncertain," and that schools applying for the discounts had "no idea what they're buying." The coalition responded, point by point. The coalition circulated the rebuttal to the cybernetwork, along with letters to the editor signed by the heads of the coalition partners. The news of Glassman's article stoked the rage of E-Rate supporters: E-mail messages pounded Congress, the FCC, the telecommunications companies, and the coalition.

In Washington, the Senate Commerce, Science & Transportation Committee held a hearing on the future of the FCC and the E-Rate program for schools and libraries. It was a bully tactic, we believed, that was designed to force the FCC's hand. The choice: kill the program or the commission, you decide. We e-mailed the cybernetwork again, urging Washington-based activists to attend the hearing and calling on out-of-towners to phone the Committee's office.

On the day of the hearing, columnist Molly Ivins of the Fort Worth *Star-Telegram* published an article that spoke for our online army and the vast majority of E-Rate supporters. She wrote, "As though determined to prove that the film 'Bulworth' has not an ounce of exaggeration in it, the powerful telecom lobby is now putting pressure on members of Congress who owe it a lot to get the industry out of the only redeeming feature of the 1996 Telecommunications Act. The phone companies are trying to weasel out of a commitment they made in '97 to subsidize the cost of connecting schools and libraries to the Internet."

Despite the innuendos made behind the scenes and reported to the coalition, the U.S. Senate hearing was surprisingly tame. By and large, members of Congress articulated their commitment to preserve the E-Rate program and the FCC. It was shocking, really: it almost appeared that Congress had gotten the message.

A Glass Half Full

On June 12, the FCC bowed—not buckled—to the pressure from Congress, the telecommunications industry, and consumer groups. In the end, the commission voted to cut the E-Rate program. It was not the result the coalition hoped for, but we took solace in what we preserved.

E-Rate services and funding were slashed by 42 percent—$1 billion in 1998—but the program remained standing. The FCC voted to distribute funds for 1998 approved E-Rate applications over 18 months—from January 1, 1998 to July 1, 1999—and to eliminate discounts for internal connections for all but the poorest schools. BellSouth and SBC Communications dropped out of the lawsuit against the E-Rate. GTE remained the lone holdout.

Without the campaign and the 22,000 messages of support and press it generated, Congress and the telecommunications companies could easily have forced the FCC to scrap the E-Rate program altogether. The cybercampaign kept them from getting what they wanted most: an easy out.

The E-Rate was, in many ways, a perfect issue for cyberadvocacy. After all, it was all about connecting kids, schools, and libraries to the Internet—a message that resonated with the cybercommunity. And, it was an e-story that clearly resonated with the press. But beyond the natural currency of the issue, the Save the E-Rate Coalition did a number of things "right" that helped build a quality campaign in cyberspace.

We built a fabulous e-mail list. The coalition list proved a strong weapon—even against the teams of high powered lawyers and lobbyists that backed the telecommunications industry. It helped to extend the influence of our organizations and our impact on Capitol Hill.

We moved quickly: forty-eight hours from campaign concept to launch. In the not-so-distant past, before cyber, our national organizations might have spent a few weeks to get word to affected members on the ground. National would call state organizations, states would call locals, locals would call members—that is, if everything went perfectly. Beyond the notification process, coalition members also expedited their organizations' customary decision-making process to ensure that it wouldn't impede the progress of our online campaign.

We were blessed with an articulate activist base that clearly understood the issue at stake, and we capitalized on that strength. Every e-mail message sent from our Web site was personally drafted by the sender—and spoke to the real impact on a school, a library, or a community. Had we required our activists to send an "officially sanctioned" message prepared by the coalition, we would have lost one of the most important qualities of our campaign: our ability to put a local face on a great big federal issue.

We took full advantage of Web technology—but we kept things simple. We designed our Web site to do one thing: generate "action." Within the span of five minutes, site visitors could get the details on the issue, identify their members of Congress, and craft and send an e-mail message to make their voice heard. Our e-mail contact capability ensured that every message sent from the site was a constituent communication—and addressed accordingly. Non-constituent e-mail has very little impact on members of Congress.

The participating organizations took a strong stand on the issue—and they recognized the value of working in coalition. Together, we were able to build a stronger campaign than any one of us could have run on our own. Our organizations' Web sites all covered the progress of the campaign. Banner ads placed on each of our sites drove traffic to the Save the E-Rate Coalition. We involved all of our e-mail networks, turned on the press machines for all of our organizations, and multiplied our organizing muscle times six. Ultimately, every organization within the larger EdLiNC coalition and an unrelated number of other groups placed the campaign banner on their Web sites and linked to the Save the E-Rate Coalition campaign site.

Our coalition supported the online campaign with a free media campaign, and turned the E-Rate story into an e-story. The press coverage helped us reach beyond our established base of cyberactivists: We heard from superintendents and school board members, educators, parents, schoolchildren, and business people. Some were our members, many were not. In all likelihood, few of these visitors to our site had ever written their members of Congress or the FCC, particularly in cyberspace. But with very few exceptions, these parents, librarians, and educators-turned-activists came to our site to send messages in support of our position. Our network and the free press were invaluable.

We kept our network plugged-in to the operations of our campaign by alerting them when new threats appeared on the horizon. In one case, our alert message actually helped bump up our e-mail count by 2,000 messages in 24 hours.

The campaign's success can be attributed to a number of elements coming together: a strong message, technology, urgency, turn-around. But ultimately, it hinged on one thing: the strength of the online community and the wired member-ships of coalition partners. In the rock-paper-scissors game, rock crushes scissors and scissors cut paper every time. In the game of Washington lobbying, grassroots efforts, backed by the power of cyberspace, can beat paid lobbyists and big money.

Chapter 7   The Lone Crusader

John Aravosis is a crusader for gay rights who also works as an Internet media and advocacy strategist in Washington, D.C. He came to Washington, as so many young people do, to work in politics. A conservative, he first worked as a legislative attorney for Republican Senator Ted Stevens (R-AK). But he eventually began to work for progressive causes, including Senator Ted Kennedy's 1994 reelection campaign and the Children's Defense Fund.

Today, Aravosis runs his own one-person consulting firm from his apartment. No longer working within an organization means having a great deal of independence. It also means having fewer resources. But the Internet is such a powerful tool that, working alone, he has been able to get national attention on a number of issues. And although he has paying clients, his greatest successes have been in promoting gay rights *pro bono*. For this cause, John Aravosis is a fierce and passionate crusader.

Living in Washington is unlike living anywhere else. An aura of power pervades the city. Politics is the air that Washingtonians breathe and national news the water they drink, and Aravosis thrives in this environment.

Building a Community for a Cause

In October 1998 far from this power center, in a Colorado hospital a gay man lay dying. Aravosis saw an AP report about the attack on Matthew Shepard, a student at the University of Wyoming, and had been moved to investigate the story. He realized that this story had aspects transcending the average crime story. He saw the story as a morality play about hatred, an object lesson about the dangers of homophobia. And he was determined that the brutal attack should become a national story—and be the basis for substantial changes in our national community and its laws.

After the attackers smashed Matthew Shepard's skull with the handle of a gun, after they drove him to another place, after they tied him to a fence and beat him again, they drove away, leaving him for dead.

But Shepard was found still alive. The person who found him lashed to a fence at first thought he was a scarecrow. He was taken to a hospital in Ft. Collins, Colorado, where he lingered in a coma for nearly a week, but he never regained consciousness. He was badly bruised over much of his body, there were multiple cuts, and inside his crushed skull was severe brain injury, enough to kill him, even without the hypothermia.

The viciousness of the attack made it clear that the motive was beyond a simple robbery. This was an execution, the victim left crucified on a fence.

Matthew Shepard was a student at the University of Wyoming. He had been open about his sexual orientation. For Aravosis, this was a clear case of a hate crime. To stop it from happening again meant to make people realize that being anti-gay has the same effect as being a racist. Hate crimes are an indication of certain groups of people being devalued by others.

The local community reacted quickly with a march in sympathy through the town as Shepard lay dying in the hospital. The police quickly found the suspects and most of the elements of the murder and did not underplay the significance of this crime. Many citizens reacted quickly to make clear that the crime, and the hatred that had prompted it, would not be tolerated. Shepard suffered alone on that first terrible night, but now the community shared his pain and his terror and chose to be by his side in spirit during the death vigil.

In a town as small as Laramie the news of the killing spread quickly. It quickly became a story of regional interest, as media in nearby cities such as Denver picked up the story. But Matthew Shepard's death did not immediately catch on as a major national story. After all, there are homicides throughout the United States all day long, every day of the year. Very few make national news.

In fact, most local stories are not considered important enough to get national attention. It depends on whether news editors and producers feel that a story will interest their readers or viewers. Newsworthiness is an odd quality, and among the variables is always the question of whether it's a "hot" news day: what else is happening?

As the local press reported the story of Matthew Shepard's death, it was quickly put out "on the wires" through the Associated Press. (The AP originated as a newspaper cooperative service formed to take advantage of the then new but costly telegraph system. Each of the newspapers would place stories "on the wires" for other member papers to use. The

Associated Press grew into a huge "wire" service. In the age of the Internet, AP now allows newspaper Web editions to carry enormous amounts of "wire" news instantly—and often electronically searchable.) As the AP story arrived in newsrooms around the country, very few news outlets gave the story much play.

But the story of Matthew Shepard's death did spread across the country, in part due to the power and breadth of the Internet. The Internet amplified the story and ensured the widespread coverage it eventually attained in the media.

After reading the story of Matthew Shepard, Aravosis immediately sent e-mail to selected journalists to make sure that they were aware of the story. Pitching a story to journalists, convincing reporters, producers and assignment editors that a story is worth attention, begins with letting them know the basic facts. Although the story had gotten play in the Rocky Mountain states, Aravosis argued that the story had national implications. He pitched several news angles: crime, legislation, human interest and gay politics. That it could be tied into ongoing coverage of human rights and hate crimes. And most of all, Aravosis argued with fervor, it was a compelling human interest story.

Of course, he wasn't the only person with a story to pitch. There are legions of public relations professionals trying to place stories. The best of them regularly get stories in the *Los Angeles Times*, *USA Today*, the *Chicago Tribune*, on Nightline and CBS Evening News, on thousands of radio stations, in *Newsweek* and *Time*, reaching tens of millions of Americans. These public relations professionals use the telephone, faxes, and power lunches to talk to key journalists. And, like Aravosis, many public relations professionals are starting to use e-mail and the Web to get their stories out, to change or reinforce public opinion, to popularize their point of view, or to put their spin on somebody else's story. And then, when the public relations people finish their pitching and spinning, the media perform a filtering process of choosing the stories they believe deserve to be made public. Unless the reporters, editors and producers are bypassed.

Aravosis decided it would be a good idea to post information about the Shepard case on a one page Web site: the "Matthew Shepard Online Resources Web site." It would perform the function of a press release. But Aravosis had more in mind for this site. It would also serve as a community building site and a place to mourn Shepard's death. For many people, the site was a shrine to Shepard, a place where anyone on the Internet could come to learn and even leave messages.

Within the first 24 hours, the Web site was contacted 50,000 times. (In the language of the Internet, that's 50,000 "hits.") By the week's end, the site would receive a half million hits. The site had become its own media outlet, with Aravosis as its publisher.

The Shepard murder became a bigger national story, with most media outlets now reporting new developments. Politicians and celebrities spoke out against the brutal incident, calling on society to become tolerant. Once a story becomes big, the news media reach out for quotes and reactions, in turn making the story bigger. And, in this era of pack journalism, news outlets legitimize the story for other outlets: if they are covering it, then others are compelled to cover it.

Almost overnight a vigil and rally was organized and held on the steps of the Capitol Building in Washington, D.C. Several senators and representatives addressed a large crowd, speaking out forcefully to condemn the killing, offering sympathy, and calling for new legislation against hate crimes. What began as an act of hatred had engendered an outpouring of hope and understanding in Laramie and far beyond.

A press release is usually a short document designed to grab attention and tell a story quickly. The"Matthew Shepard Online Resources Web site" was rich in content and reader choice. It grew as Aravosis included copies of press releases, news items, links to other sources, and messages received from around the world. Comments included heart-wrenching recollections of brutality, including stories about people who aren't gay, but were badly beaten because they seemed to fit gay stereotypes. The site also included a moving essay by Aravosis himself.

But not everything on the site was sympathetic to gays or human rights. The site's message board was used by fans of a pro wrestler to post intentionally offensive messages ridiculing supporters of gay rights. Aravosis took the message board off-line to stop the disruption caused by these messages. But he did not strip the site of messages antithetical to his point of view. Rather, the site highlighted some of the negative messages and actually pointed out various hostile Internet sites and groups that opposed gay rights. The decision to link to hostile sites and include negative material served to underscore his message: homophobia is neither shadowy nor innocuous.

But Aravosis had reasons for including links to the Family Research Council Web site and other Web sites which advocated a conservative social issue agenda. It was not part of a "feel free to shop with our competitors" ploy. Aravosis was making his site a complete resource on society's reaction to the Shepard murder and the effort to outlaw hate crimes.

In the United States and elsewhere, many small hate groups have used the Web to communicate among themselves and try to reach out to new adherents. There are numerous sites that preach against gays. Aravosis aptly used those sites to illustrate the danger faced by the gay community.

Not everyone has the same reaction to the anti-gay remarks posted to the Matthew Shepard site, but uncontrolled expressions of anger, and outrageous comments that were posted to the site generally allowed the hate-mongers to discredit themselves. By giving the haters a platform, Aravosis made it clear that for every step forward there is a chance for a step backwards.

With this site, Aravosis had become a major publisher, rivaling for a short time the reach of major newspapers and television news shows. And an odd reversal took place: media outlets asked him to link to their Web sites. Normally, a public relations person seeks an audience from media oulets. Normally, the public relations person cannot offer an audience to a news outlet. On the Web, however, the same audience that visits a major news site can also see the original press release. The only difference is that, normally, news media sites get a large amount of traffic and press release sites don't.

By spreading the word effectively, by having a compelling story, and by making the Web site more than just a simple press release, the Shepard murder site changed the rules.

On the Web, anything can be one click away. And media Web sites often enhance their news by linking to external sites, allowing readers to do their own investigating. These are often included in a separate section called "related links," which carries a warning that the site being linked is not part of the news site. And it often happens that a non-media Web site will link to a news outlet site, to allow visitors to investigate further by seeing what the press is saying. Most media sites have a reputation for being non-biased and therefore can help to legitimize the importance of an issue or the position of an organization. It is a partnership where both sites gain from their connection. This relationship is often very informal and ad hoc, each making their own decision based on their own priorities. Such cross-linking, only possible because of how the Web is designed, is very new and there are not yet any protocols.

Most of this replicates the paper world, where organizations might reprint an article to send in a packet to supporters. Organizations might mention or quote items when various radio and television broadcasts mention them. Likewise, news organizations might pull quotes from a press release or attend a press conference and include a video or audio clip in that day's new show. But for the first time the Web has allowed the two to connect directly.

What is unique in this story is news outlet sites using a source's site not just for information, but for audience as well. The many news sites depend on advertising for a significant part of their revenue. Advertising rates are practically a science in the paper and broadcast models, but they are not yet well understood on the Internet. The confusion in how to determine rates occurs even though Web sites can have more accurate readership counts than other media. For the first time, individual parts of a news medium can be charted, unlike a newspaper, for example, where there is no comprehensive measure of how many readers looked at the story on local housing on page 17 as opposed to the story about global warming on page 14. Newspaper Web sites can do precisely that, logging exact numbers of visitors to each of the two stories in today's edition.

As media sites try to establish advertising placement rates for ads, this kind of information can be incredibly useful to advertising agencies and advertisers.

In newspapers, the editor chooses which stories are to appear on the front page, just as magazines select items for the cover. On Web sites, the editors can make similar choices about placement, but there are several ways in which readers can bypass the editor's choices. One way is by having links in other sites that link directly to a particular article.

A journalist may be able to increase readership of his/her byline stories by promoting links to their stories on special interest organization sites. Individual journalists will then be able to independently show their value in increasing general readership to the whole site. Traditionally print journalists would gain prestige when editors gave their stories good placement. Now, journalists may be able to benefit even more from reader choices than from their editor's placement choices. It will be interesting to see what this does to power relationships in newsrooms.

The "Matthew Shepard Online Resources Web Site" was intended to bring attention to a serious problem in the country. And it was very successful in having the story resonate with journalists who saw this as an important story and the Web site an invaluable resource for background information. A few of the journalists who did stories on Matthew Shepard's death asked that Aravosis include a link to the article that they had written. It is likely that these requests were to help be a resource for Aravosis and not a way to drive up readership. And it is unlikely that sophisticated measuring tools have yet been developed to rate readership by the byline. But the success of non-traditional media sites to have the huge readership that Aravosis got may tempt some journalists to ask for reciprocal links to drive readership.

Journalists have often developed relationships with public relations professionals who supply them with good information and hot stories. Now that relationship could include the journalists looking for sources that can bring their own potential readership. As many media sites have found out, *Slate* magazine for example, it can be very difficult to gain an online subscriber base large enough to fund journalism. Advertising is becoming the sole source of revenue for many sites. And the advertising itself is drastically changing as it gains a brand new characteristic: a TV ad may convince you to buy a product, but it can't actually close the sale. Advertising on the Internet can through point-of-sale advertising.

As boundaries between public relations, journalism, advertising and marketing blur and dissolve, the reader faces a conundrum: how to discern any mixed motives behind what they read. The Matthew Shepard site was successful in pulling in readers, successful in helping to shape press coverage of the story and successful as a poignant monument to the murdered young man. But, despite an outpouring of support, it could not succeed in getting hate crimes legislation passed in Wyoming, or on the federal level.

Don't Ask, Don't Tell

In another case, Aravosis had great success in using the Internet media to help one individual. He has been a tireless advocate for someone who had been wronged because of his or her sexual orientation. When he heard of the story of U.S. Navy Senior Chief Petty Officer Timothy R. McVeigh (no relation to the Oklahoma City bomber), he realized that he could help by bringing attention to his story.

McVeigh had used America Online for his access to the Internet. America Online has a "profile" feature that allows users to include biographical information such as hobbies, marital status, age and other personal information. Depending on a guarantee that his identity would never be revealed, McVeigh used the word "gay" in his profile. Unfortunately for McVeigh, someone in the Navy guessed that a particular profile was his. As part of the investigation that ensued, the Navy confirmed that guess. There wasn't much to the investigation. It consisted of a single phone call to an office of America Online asking for the identity of the suspected profile. The AOL employee who fielded the call confirmed that it was indeed McVeigh's. And the Navy began its process of cashiering McVeigh.

McVeigh was one of several "outed" people who were being ousted from the military. But when Aravosis saw a plea for help over the Internet for McVeigh he saw that this story might be more compelling than others. He had an outstanding military record and Aravosis decided to work on behalf of McVeigh to help him stay in the military. First, Aravosis contacted McVeigh, using the America Online instant messaging feature that allows two users to chat in real time. Aravosis offered to help and McVeigh accepted. In this case, helping meant making a public case for McVeigh. And Aravosis decided to take advantage of the Internet to help bring attention to McVeigh's plight.

McVeigh had already been fighting the Navy's action for four months and there had been some local press coverage in Hawaii. Aravosis first helped to establish the story within the gay press, including GLORadio, a gay Internet radio show. The show's Web site stored the interview so that anyone on the Internet could listen to it at their convenience. As Aravosis worked to get the story out to the mainstream press, it was helpful to have a recorded interview that reporters and news producers could hear to determine how well McVeigh would perform as an interviewee.

Aravosis used e-mail extensively to get the story out to journalists. And the story had several hooks for the press: the problems with the military's much publicized "Don't Ask, Don't Tell" policy, the issue of privacy on the Internet, the business story of the involvement (and potential liability) of America Online—and the chance to cover the Internet as a cultural phenomenon in which people can use the Internet to communicate in presumed anonymity.

Avarosis stressed that the story "had legs." Still ahead was America Online's response, the Navy's fight against the charge of illegal searches, and the trial itself.

Once Aravosis started to push it, the story took off. All of the major newspapers and television networks covered the story, despite the unfortunate confusion caused by McVeigh's name, which was also the name of the Oklahoma City bomber.

Aravosis triumphed. Within weeks of his entry into the case, America Online did something Aravosis said AOL had not previously done: It told its members (that is, its clients) what had happened in the McVeigh case, explaining how McVeigh's privacy was invaded. Later that same month, a judge ordered the Navy to reinstate McVeigh.

The Navy had lost, but it was short of unconditional surrender. The Navy kept up its efforts against McVeigh, and six months later reached a compromise with him. McVeigh accepted an honorable discharge, with full pension. The military did not change its policy and the President did not publicly weigh in against the clear violation of his own policy.

When Did the Thesaurus Become Extinct?

"How does a word get into the dictionary?" Merriam-Webster has a simple answer: usage.

To decide which words go into the dictionary and what those words mean, Merriam-Webster editors study usage: which words people use and how they use them.

In theory, it has long been an interactive process: the dictionary maker researches usage among speakers and writers (often taking decades to produce a new edition), then speakers and writers consult the dictionary for information on usage (often using the same edition for decades). Today, because of the Internet, that interaction is exponentially faster. This has dramatically altered the relationship of the resource and the reader.

Despite Merriam-Webster's long-standing scholarly approach to gathering and recording actual usage (describing, not prescribing), they have succumbed to political pressure in the era of political correctness.

They have a policy of eliminating derogatory epithets for certain groups. Even though those slurs are in fact used by large numbers of speakers of the English language, it is widely understood that society has a valid interest in discouraging the discriminatory use of these words.

Dictionaries are considered to be the final arbitrator of correctness, despite the fact that they only mirror how words are used. As new words are coined, dictionary and thesaurus editors normally only include them if they are likely to survive, not on moral or aesthetic grounds. But, with the advent of spell checkers and thesauruses in word processors and online reference materials, technology has closed the gap between recording usage and checking correctness. The power of these electronic tools has changed the possibilities of how language is used. For better or for worse, the role of dictionary and thesaurus have changed.

Merriam-Webster's dictionary and thesaurus are very visible to the online users both through their Web site and their America Online presence. And that was how John McMullen, a gay rights activist and radio broadcaster, found that the synonyms listed for the word "homosexual" included "faggot" and other demeaning terms. Startlingly, the list of related words included "pederast," which means someone (regardless of gender orientation) who has sex with a child. McMullen called Aravosis to help in bringing pressure to change the thesaurus. Aravosis, working with McMullen, immediately brought these to the attention of the press, to America Online and to G & C Merriam Company, which owns Merriam-Webster.

A year earlier, the NAACP criticized the Merriam-Webster dictionary for using "black person" as the definition for the word "nigger."[1] Merriam-Webster changed its policy for inclusion of words that could be considered demeaning, but it had not applied this policy change to words related to gays and lesbians. Now, within days of Aravosis complaining, the online thesaurus was pulled off America Online. And soon the entries were changed.

Merriam-Webster editors were in the uncomfortable position of being directly (and successfully) lobbied to change for political reasons what had been a scholarly decision.

Aravosis has been a champion of gay causes who, by under-standing the capabilities and dynamics of the Internet, has been able to influence the media and how the media works. He has taken stories that might have been ignored and made them front page, changed the relationship of journalists to their sources, and even altered the reference tools reporters use.

---

[1] NAACP press release, October 14, 1997. *www.naacp.org/president/ releases/archives/1997/diction.htm*

Chapter 8

Congress Approaches
the 21st Century

"We're in the communications business"
        ...said Congresswoman Anna Eshoo (D-CA).

And business is booming!
        ...she might have added.

When John Quincy Adams sat in the House of Representatives, citizens could communicate with their congressman in person or by mail. When they wrote, Adams took up his quill and wrote back to them.

When John Kennedy served in the House more than a century later, his constituents could communicate in person, by mail (or telegram), or by phone. And Kennedy had a staff to help handle the telephone calls and correspondence.

Half a century later, Congresswoman Eshoo's voters can talk to her in person and can communicate with her by mail, telegram and phone, as well. But there are also faxes and the Internet. And the volume of corre-spondence can get so heavy when an issue like the 1998 impeachment debate reaches its climax that even her staff can't keep up with it.

On one day during the impeachment debate, Eshoo's office received more than one hundred phone calls, 30 faxes, 50 letters or postcards, and 1,000 electronic messages on the issue, each of which needed a reply.

Information and communication are air and water for members of Congress, who have to write and vote on legislation dealing with everything from agriculture and abortion to pollution, roads, military spending and gun control — while representing citizens with strong opinions on all sides of nearly all issues. It takes a lot of communication back and forth between citizens and legislators. And members of Congress who don't manage that communication well are hurting their chances of being reelected.

The Internet has created the potential of nearly infinite amounts of information and constant, even overwhelming, communication. The impeachment process gave the first clear evidence of the massive impact the Internet can have on the level of congressional correspondence. Because the old ways of accepting messages and responding to constituents proved inadequate to the task, Congress has been forced to find better ways to cope. The two main problems to solve were making sure that all messages get through to Congress and enabling congressional offices to be able to manage and respond to large increases in correspondence. The technology that has helped to make it easier for citizens to contact Congress is also helping to provide solutions to dealing with the increased volume.

A high percentage of correspondence to Congress is sent in as a result of organized grassroots efforts. Over the years, grassroots techniques have developed, with the goal of swamping congressional offices with constituent messages. Tried and true techniques include signed petitions, postcard

campaigns, coordinated phone calls, or printed letters generated for a particular issue. Both for individual correspondence
and organized grassroots efforts, the Internet lowered the
barriers for citizens to send a message to Congress.

Although there is no significant difference in the effort to
write an e-mail or a letter, it is easier to send the e-mail. After
writing a letter, the sender must address, stamp—and pay for
the stamp—and find a mailbox. If a news story gets you mad,
it only takes moments for you to send an e-mail to Congress.
The extra effort involved for people in using the Postal
Service means fewer letters are sent, especially among people
who are already more used to e-mail. The barrier to sending
an e-mail can be close to zero, assuming that one has regular
access to a computer and a modem.

In a grassroots campaign, a group takes the initiative to coax
others into taking action. Using the Internet can decrease the
cost of reaching a wide group of people, and because the
Internet can make it easier to take action, the potential for
wider participation is considerable. With techniques like "e-
mail your friends our message" and easy to sign online
petitions on Web sites, Congress is only a click away for
grassroots supporters.

One thing that did not change with the introduction of messages through the Internet is the importance of communication. There is a misconception that members of Congress
discount e-mail and Web-based messages. Each Congressman
evaluates messages differently. Part of that evaluation is how
the message relates to beliefs that they hold. Members of
Congress are not blank slates on which constituent messages
always imprint an outlook and action. Nor are constituent

messages the only input into Congressional consciousness; there is lobbying, media reports, and Congressional staff research. But constituents' messages do make an impact, whether they come by post or by e-mail.

How great the impact is may vary. Members of Congress may be likelier to discount messages that seem manufactured and insincere. The common term for this pseudo-grassroots communication is "Astroturf." The amount of effort that goes into composing and sending the message may impress upon the Congressman its importance to the sender. An incomprehensible postcard that arrives among thousands of others may not make as much impact as one clear handwritten (and heartfelt) letter.

Members of Congress are generally most receptive to messages from their own constituents. Their constituents are the ones that elected them to office and (more to the point) can vote against them in the next election. But because the Internet has made it so much easier and cheaper to write to multiple members of Congress, it is likely that an overwhelming majority of e-mail messages a congressional office receives will be from outside of their congressional district.[1] Congressional offices will often separate out messages from outside their district, whether the messages are electronic or paper. Sorting is based on the postal address including the ZIP code, so those messages that fail to include this information (easily omitted in e-mail) will not be treated as constituent messages.

---

[1] Bonner and Associates/American University: Survey on Congressional Use of the Internet. Washington, D.C.

Each method of corresponding has its own characteristics that influence how it is received. A phone call demands immediate attention; a phone campaign can overwhelm an office's ability to do other business. A postcard campaign can generate bulky post office trays of cards. Do they indicate strongly felt, widespread support for a point of view? Or are they just a measure of an organization's ability to coax people to fill in a postcard?

Internet messages come in quickly and silently. And because of the newness of the medium, many members of Congress are just now beginning to think about them as part of the communications process. Congressional offices have a more difficult time telling individually written e-mail messages from cookie cutter e-mail campaigns, because there are fewer clues as compared with paper-based communications, where handwriting looks different from printing, hand addressed envelopes look different than mass addressed envelopes, and signatures look different from typed names.

It isn't surprising that Congresswoman Anna Eshoo pioneered using the Internet to communicate with her constituents. Her district, which lies between San Francisco and San Jose, is the heart of Silicon Valley. The people who live here are among the most Internet aware in the world. And they were not likely to put up with a representative who did not use their favored means of communication. She was one of the first members of Congress to accept e-mail, calling it "another very important way for people to talk to me," a comment that reflects the great weight she places on messages from her district.

A high percentage of members of Congress followed Eshoo's lead, accepting electronic mail and recognizing it as a vital and growing aspect of constituent communication.

Communications Overload

Although members of Congress accept e-mail, that's not the same thing as being able to cope with it. After the release of the Starr report, the electronic messages to Congress began to pour in. Millions of them. Half a million messages came through the anti-impeachment "Censure and Move On" campaign's Web site. Other sites, including Roger Hedgecock's pro-impeachment Web-site, accounted for hundreds of thousands more. America Online subscribers could use the service to send e-mail to Congress directly from within impeachment news stories. And there were hundreds of other Web sites that also included an easy way to contact Congress. People who felt the impulse to write Congress after hearing a radio or television news story also used the Internet to contact Congress. And friends e-mailed each other with information on how to contact Congress. The tens of millions of Internet users all had easy and inexpensive access to contacting Congress within seconds. Between the coordinated grassroots campaigns and individual interest, citizens let Congress know where they stood.

Citizens sending millions of messages to Congress is not, however, the same thing as Congress receiving millions of messages. As with any other delivery method, e-mail overload can clog the ability of Congress to receive it. During the deluge of messages for and against impeachment, there were several points of failure. The first was at the sending end, where Web sites or e-mail servers were overloaded. Not all of the systems set up to transmit the messages could handle the unexpectedly heavy load. And the systems that receive the messages within Congress could not always handle the load. It is impossible to know how much was lost, but it was likely to have been a substantial percentage during certain periods of high traffic.

Most communications systems are designed to cope well with a fairly high percentage of the estimated peak usage. But many systems will falter when the usage goes beyond a certain point. Sometimes during phone campaigns directed at Congress, the Capitol phone system is stressed and sometimes fully saturated. At that point, no additional calls can come in.

This syndrome often afflicts Internet-based systems. Avoiding these logjams is made difficult by the high cost of resources needed to handle peak traffic levels. Because the decision to spend on increasing capacity of any system (phones, roads, airports, polling stations, restaurant staffing for Mother's Day, etc.) is often based on past experience, the newness of the Internet and its rapid expansion make projection of future demand highly speculative.

Just as necessity is the mother of invention, improvement is often the byproduct of failure. The Senate and the House of Representatives failed to handle the load caused by the huge volume of impeachment e-mail. The mess led to political pressure within Congress to upgrade the system. Since the deluge, the House has installed a system better equipped to handle higher peak loads. This is not a unique story. It echoes what has been happening elsewhere in the public and private sectors (such as the inability of online tax preparation sites to handle the crush of last minute filers, or the recent series of outages at online brokerage firms).

Even though the overload of the e-mail infrastructure meant that congressional offices didn't get all the messages addressed to them, the number of e-mail messages that did get through was huge. And that was in addition to the mail, faxes and phone messages. The ability of congressional offices to deal with the onslaught of messages was sorely stressed, even in the best run offices.

In the Trenches

Each congressional office made daily and weekly tallies of how many constituents wanted the President impeached, how many wanted him to resign, how many thought censure was sufficient, and how many just wanted the whole impeachment process to end. But dealing with such a large volume of correspondence was difficult.

It was not the first time that huge numbers of messages had been received on Capitol Hill. Four years earlier, the NAFTA (North American Free Trade Agreement) debate had prompted an ocean of letters and faxes (and only a small number of e-mail messages to the few offices that had a public e-mail address). But this time, e-mail was a major part of the mix. And offices were not at all prepared.

The House of Representatives first allowed Members to accept e-mail in 1993. There had been a test with a handful of offices prior to the general release of the capability. The proposed rules for accepting e-mail had at one point included the need for the constituent to register by postcard. Although that and other quirky rules fell by the wayside, the e-mail system is still going through change and updating. Although e-mail and other Internet correspondence is now an established form of communication, the process of accepting and re-sponding is in a transition phase from a paper-based world to an electronic one.

Congressional offices receive huge amounts of mail, phone calls, and faxes almost year round. Each day there are five deliveries of mail, some deliveries over a foot thick and weighing over ten pounds. Then there are the bicycle couriers with packages, express mail, reports from the Library of Congress, Western Union telegrams, visitors with handouts. Just opening, date stamping, and sorting the load can be a day long job.

Some members of Congress respond with letters to most or all incoming messages. Some offices only respond to written communications. Some offices do not respond to postcard campaigns. But in most cases, reports are made to the congressman to let him know what the constituents are saying. One of the primary responsibilities of a congressional office is to track and respond to constituent correspondence. Congressional offices usually have about two people assigned full time to drafting responses and managing the response system.

Unlike the ease with which the Internet allows people to send messages to Congress, the process of responding is laborious. The systems to handle correspondence were designed to handle postal responses. The writing of one response letter may span one to three weeks, depending on how long it takes to get all the information to make an informed response. And usually the drafting and approval process means that the letter may travel among several of the staff and the congressman. Although most offices now use a computer system to track correspondence and write and print the responses, it is a very paper intensive process.

Most members of Congress respond to their constituents by printing a letter and sending it through the mail.[2] Responses to e-mail are also printed out. All responses are sent out to the constituents by mail, no matter how the constituent originally contacted the office, whether by phone, postcard, letter, and telegram or through the Internet.

At the time of the impeachment, some technologies had already been instituted in Congress to add speed and efficiency to the process of dealing with messages through the Internet. Additionally, technology was put in place to allow members of Congress to respond through the Internet. The flood of messages due to the impeachment accelerated the effort to improve that technology and deploy it widely. Although members of Congress might want to take the messages contained in e-mail seriously, they might not get the chance if their offices are unable to process the huge volume coming in. Internet technology had made it easier to send messages and technology would help Congress respond.

A Glimmer of Hope

There were five main problems that had to be solved in order for Congress to be able to cope with the increasing stream of messages through the Internet.

- The first was to make sure that the messages can get through to Congress.

---

[2] Members of Congress do not have free use of mail through the franking privilege (which allows them to use signatures, rather than stamps). The rates they pay are the same as a commercial firm, and the cost is taken from their annual budget.

- The second was to help constituents find their member of Congress on the Internet.

- The third was to allow members of Congress to sort through incoming electronic mail to find the messages from their own constituents.

- The fourth was to integrate the processing of e-mail efficiently into the overall office systems.

- The fifth was to use the Internet to send responses for messages that are received through the Internet.

To help constituents find their member of Congress, the House of Representatives created a "Write Your Representative" Web page. The page allows people to find their congressman by entering their own home ZIP code. The system would then bring the person to a page that allowed them to put their message in a Web form. The information would then be delivered by e-mail to participating congressional offices.

This also served to largely solve the third problem. Because the House of Representatives Web site automatically routed messages on the basis of the sender's home ZIP code, the offices receiving these e-mail messages would be relatively sure that the messages were from their own district.

At the same time, the leading vendor of correspondence systems to Congress, a company then called Intelligent Solutions, worked with Congresswoman Eshoo to develop a system that allowed constituents to send messages through the Eshoo Web site. These messages would be transferred out of the normal e-mail system directly into the correspondence system in the congressional office. The process of responding could be handled electronically and the response would be posted on the Web site in a way that would be accessible to the constituent who had sent the message. Intelligent Solutions called this system CitizenDirect and almost a hundred congressional offices adopted it.

Unfortunately, both Write Your Representative and CitizenDirect had a major drawback: neither could accept regular e-mail. The systems were also incompatible with other Web sites that were designed to forward messages as e-mail messages.

Some congressional offices substituted one of these systems as a way of receiving messages through the Internet instead of accepting regular e-mail. Many of those offices felt that they could not handle the level of e-mail that they were receiving because so much of it wasn't from their own district.

There was awareness on Capitol Hill that congressional offices were going to need better technology as the volume of incoming messages continued to increase with the growth of the Internet. Although the impeachment was an anomaly, and it is infrequent that an issue gets hot enough to create that extraordinary level of public involvement, the growth of the Internet (and grassroots action using the Internet) will in all likelihood allow the total volume of congressional correspondence to grow exponentially.

Intelligent Solutions, now called ACS Desktop Solutions, recognizing the need to replace CitizenDirect with a system that was open to regular e-mail messages as well as messages sent from a Web page, introduced IMA (Internet Mail Agent). It would retain a tight integration with the correspondence system that their congressional customers used and would enable congressional offices to respond with e-mail messages. In this way, congressional offices could continue to draft responses for the messages in a system that could efficiently handle the growing Internet traffic. This system is just now being rolled out to congressional offices.

The hope is that Congress can handle an increasing e-mail load, and as a result be better able to listen to the people it represents. Grassroots organizations are stepping up efforts to utilize the Internet to gain adherents and influence policy. Normal correspondence may increase by a factor of ten — or even a hundred. For some time into the future, Congress will have to run hard to keep from falling behind the people in the use of the Internet.

Chapter 9

Virtually Walking the Precinct

Campaigning in the Digital Age

When Senator Bob Dole announced his campaign Web site address during a nationally televised debate in 1996, it was a clear indication that campaign Web sites would become a required part of any legitimate political campaign. With the success of Jesse Ventura's Internet aided campaign for Minnesota governor and Steve Forbes' online presidential candidacy announcement, it cemented the importance of the Internet. Just as President Lyndon Johnson effectively used television spots 35 years ago to campaign, candidates are now starting to buy banner ads on media Web sites.

Campaign Web sites have been evolving from information repositories to becoming virtual campaign organizations. At first, the sites would include information similar to what is printed in campaign brochures. Now the sites are coming closer to mirroring the entire campaign organization, including posting position papers and media alerts, coordinating volunteers, collecting donations and selling campaign paraphernalia.

Campaigns are ad hoc organizations that exist for short periods of time, have one short term goal (or two if the primary allows) and lots of unpaid or underpaid volunteers doing much of the work. As Internet technology is incorporated into campaigns, it creates more stable organizations by filling in the gaps, and helping organize the numbers of volunteers. With a campaign's constant creation of press releases, leaflets and other documents, their consolidation on the Internet can make access easier than the normal mad search through boxes and hastily organized file cabinets.

The Internet presence of the campaign has allowed supporters to be instantly plugged in. Campaigns often struggle to reach out or correspond to potential campaign activists and supporters. Using online volunteer self service sections and instant e-mail alerts has meant that no one who has access to the Internet feels left out. And the opportunity to distribute campaign buttons, bumper stickers and other gear through the Internet helps to further bind supporters to the campaign.

Maintaining a campaign Web site can vary in price. But it is possible to create a simple one for practically nothing. Today, there is almost no excuse for not having a campaign Web site. Even in municipal elections, savvy candidates are posting sites and offering an e-mail address. Whereas buying advertising can be very expensive, especially on television, the Internet offers an affordable adjunct.

Gubernatorial candidate Peter Vallone lost his 1998 bid to unseat New York Governor George Pataki. But he did run an interesting Internet banner ad campaign. A study of the effects of the ads posted on Web media sites indicated that ads could sway voters. The study measured a seven percent change in people's perception of Governor Pataki.

The study found "Pataki's favorability ratings were 7 points lower among the EXPOSED cell compared to the CONTROL cell. This finding alone is statistically significant at a 95% confidence level. This finding is further bolstered by the fact that the data also shows a 7 point increase in Pataki's unfavorable ratings."[1]

To buy media on the Internet is to test uncharted waters, as the field of advertising on the Internet is only recently becoming somewhat standardized. And in the case of the Vallone campaign, it was used only as a way to inexpensively reach voters in an election where Pataki had much more money to spend. But it is possible to guess how to reach an audience and do selected ad placements. The potential for highly targeted media campaigns is great, possibly allowing ads to appear for particular readers visiting a media site. It is also another opportunity for candidates to use banner ads for negative campaigning.

Until sound and video on the Internet become more common and increase in quality, it is unlikely that campaign ads will have the emotional pull that is possible on television and radio. When President Lyndon Johnson's campaign created the provocative "Daisy" television spot, which started with a young girl counting flower petals and ended with a countdown to an atomic explosion, it was clear that television could create the punch that would knock viewers over. Campaigns can be won or lost on television. The Internet is a much harder sell.

---

[1] E-Voter 98: Measuring the Impact of Online Advertising for a Political Candidate. January 1999. *www.e-voter98.com/overview.html*

A New Playing Field

There are three major fields of combat in elections: the area controlled directly by a candidate, including Web sites, campaign ads, and printed material; the media, where candidates can hope to influence articles and editorials; and the playing field where candidates meet each other and compete one-on-one. Debates, town halls, and other open forums are the playing field where candidates are most exposed and often directly confront their opponents.

Debates can be quite memorable, for their eloquence, for their foibles, and for the exposure of the real character of the candidates. The Lincoln-Douglas debates proved the importance of debates in elections. The Kennedy-Nixon televised debate showed the need to be skilled with media technology. For challengers the debate can be the best opportunity to best the incumbent. And for the incumbents and front runners debates can be potential disasters.

The openness of the Internet provides an opportunity to expand the debate beyond the normal confines of strict time limits. The Internet is capable of allowing a wider range of candidates to participate, to allow wider participation of the audience and to include races that may have been left out of other media coverage.

DemocracyNet is a pioneering organization in online political forums. DemocracyNet describes itself as a voters' guide, but it is much more. DemocracyNet fills the gaps left by other media which don't have the time for sponsoring open and free ranging debates.

Generally, online voter guides are a crucial new addition to elections, allowing volumes of information to be collected on candidates. This can include Federal Elections Campaign contribution data, biographies of the candidates, past votes, endorsements, contact information, and general information about voter registration and polling places.

Voter guides can be neutral, offering information in a straight-forward way. Vote Smart is a voluminous guide that offers wide ranging data on candidates throughout the country. Open Secrets is a Web site of the Center for Responsive Politics that has revolutionized the use of candidates' contri-bution reports to the Federal Election Commission. Because the reports are obtainable in electronic formats, it makes it easier to post them to the Web. Open Secrets takes the reports and makes them easy to search in order to find patterns in contributions to candidates.

Some voter guides are issue oriented and can provide a particular perspective on candidates. The League of Conserva-tion Voters offers a polished site that offers assessments of elected officials based on their voting history on environmen-tal issues. Between both types of guides, voters can make well informed choices based on their own preferences. And Web based voter guides offer voters day long access, which can come in handy the morning of the election.

DemocracyNet has created a voter's guide that allows candi-dates, local organizations, and citizens to participate in shaping and adding to the site. DemocracyNet has created a technological solution that allows it or a hosting local organi-zation to set up an election area on its site. DemocracyNet has established a relationship with the League of Women Voters and its affiliates and other organizations to provide the expertise in knowing the particulars in local elections and setting a framework for candidates and the public to partici- pate. Candidates in turn are given password access to be able to add content under their own names on the site.

The issues section is arranged in a grid with the candidates and issues as the headings. If the candidates choose to add their own comments, there is a link to it from the grid. The grid can expand to include additional topics. As topics are added the candidates are alerted to the question and can respond.

Visitors to the site have the opportunity to learn a great deal about the candidates. And if they feel that there are additional issues that need to be raised, they can raise them. A candidate can choose to respond or not.

DemocracyNet is changing elections. Area Madaras, director of DemocracyNet related the story of one campaign where last minute issues were covered directly by the candidates. In the Los Angeles area there was a local school board election where candidates had been participating in DemocracyNet's site. Just ten days before an election there was news of tainted strawberries being served in public schools. Food safety is not always the top or most pressing issue in school board elections, but concerned parents wanted to make sure it was addressed.

Because DemocracyNet's site allowed citizen participation, people e-mailed questions to school board candidates. Candidates responded to the issue of food safety, allowing the public in a relatively short period of time to absorb the various positions and factor it into their voting.

In the Florida gubernatorial election, the Florida League of Women Voters in conjunction with DemocracyNet helped to ensure that the front runner would not be able to avoid his challenger. Republican Jeb Bush was the clear favorite over Democrat Buddy McKay in the race. Jeb Bush had already set up a comprehensive Web site that served to help activate his supporters. Both candidates had been invited to participate in the DemocracyNet Web site.

Less than a couple weeks out from the election, Buddy McKay posted his position on certain issues to the DemocracyNet site. Jeb Bush's campaign responded almost immediately after being alerted that McKay had posted to the DemocracyNet site. And then things snowballed into a vigorous online debate that included ten issues brought up by the two candidates: an unusual unscheduled debate in the waning days of the campaign.

While some congressional elections can get poor media coverage, municipal elections can be completely lost in the mix. Most elections seem to be about the top of the ticket, whether presidential, gubernatorial or other statewide elections. DemocracyNet has allowed every election to have whatever space it needs, giving it a full airing and allowing full access.

Allowing full access has also meant giving equal coverage to third party candidates.

DemocracyNet allows all candidates to participate in its site and, in so doing, has tried to enhance television debates by bringing participation by candidates that are not included in the broadcast segments to simultaneously answer questions by posting to its site. To augment the *Los Angeles Times* sponsored televised gubernatorial debate in 1998, DemocracyNet had questions transcribed and sent by e-mail to candidates. The candidates were allowed two hours within which to post their written responses to the questions. The tight deadline offered at least some of the spontaneity that live television creates. Although the television audience may have been larger, many people at least had the opportunity to see a wider spectrum of discussion. DemocracyNet also posted the full transcription of the television debate along with the online portion. In that way, the debate could be referred to and read throughout the election.

Using the Internet as a debate forum means that candidates will need to hone their online skills. Much like debaters have learned to wear dark suits for television appearances, a new type of debating skills will have to be developed to succeed in this new medium. Perhaps it will hearken back to the openness and freewheeling nature of the Lincoln-Douglas debates.

Playing with Matching Funds

The growth of commerce over the Internet has been astonishing. By entering the 20 numbers that comprise a credit card number and expiration date, it is possible to purchase airline tickets, groceries, antiques, business suits and coffee. The ease of using credit cards for secure purchasing has meant that for the time being it is the coin of the Internet realm.

Although it would be lovely if money were not a huge factor in elections, it is often a critical factor. That political advertisements can change opinion is part and parcel of campaign strategy; however, effectively getting a message out depends on reaching voters. Television and radio ads are often the best way to reach voters with a message. But buying media is expensive. For this reason, fund raising has grown in importance. Also, with a cap on contributions to candidates running for federal office, it is necessary to have sophisticated fund raising tactics to reach enough willing contributors.

Currently candidates have access to technology that allows them to collect money from contributors over the Internet but the overall level of sophistication pales with the phone and direct mail fund raising campaigns. Candidates have included sections on their campaign Web sites that include directions on how to contribute either by mail or through the Web site. In phone and mail solicitation, the contact is initiated by the campaign. Fund raisers can get lists of potential contributors, especially those who have contributed in the past to other candidates in previous elections.

Contacting people over the Internet usually entails sending e-mail. However, the attitude that many people and the press have regarding proactive campaigns is much harsher for proactive e-mail than for regular mail or phone calls. And the list development for e-mail is not yet at the same level of sophistication as phone numbers and street addresses. Campaigns are still struggling to find ways to bring in more money, and they are searching for ways to better take advantage of the Internet.

At the top of every 1040 IRS tax form there is a place to check if you want public money to be given to presidential candidates. The money collected is then disbursed to candidates who meet certain requirements that the Federal Election Committee (FEC), sets out in its regulations. Within these rules the FEC matches contributions made to presidential candidates.

One of the rules against matching those contributions was if the contributions were made by credit card. In principal, a credit card payment is not a transfer of money from the contributor's own assets but rather a loan which may or may not be repaid. The FEC would only recognize a contribution as eligible for generating matching funds if it was made with a written instrument, such as a check. This would create a paper trail that would include signatures on the payments, which are used as legal proof. In that credit card transactions are the easiest and fastest way for a visitor to a Web site to transmit money and that any transaction done over the Internet is inherently not paper based, the FEC rules blocked matching contributions made to presidential campaigns.

The year 2000 presidential election is likely to be a break-through year for election contributions, because more people are connected to the Internet and online commerce has become standard.

In 1999, former U.S. Senator and basketball star Bill Bradley took on Vice President Al Gore in the race for the Democratic nomination for President. Bill Bradley needed to raise some serious cash to be a serious contender. Bradley established a campaign Web site that included a contribution page to accept money from his supporters. Since the FEC regulations precluded matching those contributions, it meant Bradley would, in a sense, be losing money by raising it through the Internet. So his campaign sent a request to the FEC to recon-sider the regulations.

The FEC was put in the unenviable position of seeming like a backward, moribund bureaucracy. In the case of online contributions, to block matching funds would mean to diminish the role of the small campaign contributor.

The FEC made the decision that, although new regulations would need to be written to ensure adequate audit trails for Internet transactions, candidates would be able to get matching funds for online contributions. So Bradley fired the shot that made using the Internet a legitimate avenue for raising presidential contributions.

It is too early to know whether online contributions will be more than a small fraction of overall contributions. But the potential will mean that Internet savvy fund raisers will hone the techniques necessary for cajoling contributions from a broad Internet audience.

Chapter 10

Take Action Now

The *e-advocates* Plan for Building an Online Campaign

Getting Started

At some point, all activists reach the decision point. After surfing the Web, checking out the competition, reading a book or an article, attending a conference—or staring down a legislative threat—the moment arrives. It is the moment when the risk of waiting seems greater than the risk of taking an action. It's time to take that first step into cyberspace.

Cyberadvocacy, the act of advocating online, can be as simple as sending an e-mail to a legislator or as complex as launching a major Internet-based campaign. The scope of the activity is defined—not by what the other person is doing or what the latest bells and whistles are on the Net—but rather by the overall advocacy goal.

Like any grassroots advocacy tool, the Internet has its limitations. For example, a public Web site isn't the place to post the private strategic information about your campaign. The Internet isn't a replacement for a personal visit with your representative. Sometimes, nothing is more effective in persuading a member of Congress to your way of thinking than the sound of his staffers' telephones ringing off the hook with constituent calls. As with all grassroots advocacy tools, the

Internet's advocacy impact is directly related to the issue, the timing, the legislator, and the constituency.

The driving force behind successful Internet advocacy campaigns isn't computer code or flashing graphics on a Web site. It's knowing when and how to use the medium to advance the cause. The first step in gaining this knowledge is to understand the strengths and limitations of the tools.

The World Wide Web

Technically speaking, the Web is a global, crosslinked database of text, pictures, graphics, animation, and sound. Users can navigate the Web by clicking their computer mouse at the location of hyperlinks—links to parts of a site or other sites on the World Wide Web. The Web can search out and retrieve information on demand.

Politically speaking, a Web site can supercharge the speed and power of your advocacy campaign. As the Cancer March organizers demonstrated, a good Web site can serve as the virtual headquarters for an off-line activity, providing the online database tools for supporters to volunteer, delivering logistical information for an event, and more.

It can also be the launch pad for an overnight virtual political demonstration. "Censure and Move On" organized its campaign almost exclusively in cyberspace. The campaign had no off-line organization, no fancy offices, and a no frills budget. But the organizers did have a specific, measurable, advocacy goal: to gather signatures online for a petition that urged Congress to censure President Clinton and move on. This flash campaign's Web site served as the sole organizing mechanism and implementation scheme to achieve the goal. Users or surfers could visit the site, sign, and send the online petition, or they could do more. Visitors could volunteer to act as a spokesperson for the campaign, telephone Congress, "tell a friend" and encourage them to participate, and make an online pledge of money or volunteer hours to defeat impeachment supporters running for reelection in 2000. Reporters covering the campaign could check the site for the latest counts of petition signers, and volunteer hours and funds pledged. The site was the headquarters for all key aspects of the campaign.

As "Censure and Move On" and the Cancer March demonstrated, a Web site is a valuable resource for an advocacy campaign. But, it isn't the end-all. That's because Web sites are essentially passive instruments. A Web site can't knock on the door (or the desktop) of a potential activist. A Web site hangs in cyberspace, waiting for the next visitor. Once the visitor arrives, a Web site can offer many tools and applications to entice the Web surfer to action. But the supporter has to find the Web site first.

E-mail

E-mail is perhaps the single, most effective online advocacy tool, largely because it is inherently proactive. E-mail transmits a message from one Internet user to another. It gives activists the ability to knock on the desktop of potential supporters. In its simplest form, e-mail is sent from one e-mail box to another. When online activists collect e-mail addresses, they can enter the e-mail address into an online address book. Or, an activist can use the magic of e-mail list software to compile an automated list, sometimes called a listserv. Listservs enable your potential supporters to send an e-mail to a specific e-mail address, type a message in the subject line (based on certain specifications required by your software), and automatically subscribe or remove themselves from your list. Many organizations and campaigns also include features on their Web site that enable supporters to join their e-mail lists by filling out a Web form that updates the database of supporters' e-mail addresses.

E-mail lists are the real engine for activism on the Internet. Activist networks, such as the Save the E-Rate Coalition, use "announcement" e-mail lists to quickly and cheaply communicate their advocacy message out to many supporters simultaneously. These lists are designed to communicate on a one-to-many basis. Save the E-Rate activists could not, for example, read the coalition's alert message and send an e-mail reply to the entire online activist list.

"Discussion" e-mail lists allow two-way communication between users on a list, or many-to-many communication. Subscribers to the discussion list send messages to a specific address that, in turn, sends their message to all of the users on the list. Discussion lists can be valuable tools for building an online relationship between and among various supporters of your advocacy campaign. Depending on the objectives of your advocacy and your discussion list, it can be a home for freewheeling debate on a variety of topics or specifically geared to advance your advocacy goal. OMB Watch, an organization whose mission includes advancing nonprofit's capacity to effectively use technology, hosts an excellent discussion list for the nonprofit community on Internet issues, including topics of online advocacy and community building. To join, or simply review the posting to this discussion list, visit *www.ombwatch.org.*

Many discussion mailing lists are "moderated." That is, the list is managed by a designated individual. Depending on the list, the moderator can receive all incoming messages to ensure that they are focused on the relevant topic for discussion and forward on only appropriate ones to subscribers. Or, the moderator may have the responsibility for determining who can or can't join the list.

As the Save the E-Rate campaign and the American Civil Liberties Union's cyberadvocacy program illustrated, e-mail lists are the backbone of strong online advocacy. But building your own e-mail list isn't the only way to knock on doors in cyberspace.

As ACLU and other groups have effectively shown, the e-mail lists of other organizations and groups can be a valuable springboard for supporting your efforts. Online activists need to identify those mailing lists whose audiences share an interest in the advocacy issue they are advancing and then learn and abide by the rules of the road for posting messages to the list. There are literally tens of thousands of lists on the Internet today, and many resource books—and several Web sites—devoted exclusively to the subject of identifying and posting messages to them.

Newsgroups and Discussion Boards

Newsgroups and discussion boards are cyber style bulletin boards where Internet users post their messages for viewing by others in the online community. There are tens of thousands of newsgroups and bulletin boards that exist on the Internet. The USENET news system is one of the oldest and largest newsgroup technologies. USENET news sites distribute these bulletin-board messages across the Internet, and subscribers may access the newsgroup bulletins from their desktop. In addition, many online newspapers and Internet providers offer similar bulletin boards that enable visitors to comment on a news story, event, or other area of interest on their site. The topics cover the gamut. In all likelihood, there is already a newsgroup or discussion board that deals with the issue you want to advance online. Once you identify the newsgroups and boards that address your areas of interest, you have a great avenue to publish your views to a wide audience of potential supporters of your issue and to learn what others are saying and thinking about the topic.

Forums, Chatrooms, and Online Conferences

More and more Web sites and commercial services are providing the tools and the space for Internet users to engage in live conversations online. These venues offer online organizers several important opportunities.

It is possible, for example, to host live chats on your own Web site, enabling site visitors to discuss your advocacy issue with knowledgeable sources—such as organization heads, members of the legislature, and so on. If you have a Web site and the tools, you can sponsor an online debate with candidates for elective office to determine their views on issues of concern to your supporters or members.

Even if you don't have a Web site, you can certainly participate in one of the chats or conferences already taking place in cyberspace. Forums, chats, and online conferences—especially those on topics related to your advocacy goal—give you the opportunity to urge potential supporters in a real-time format to take an action in support of your issue. And if your advocacy issue is on the front page of the newspaper, it's very likely that there is a chat or conference taking place online.

Your job, as a cyberorganizer, is to find those spaces where live chats are taking place, whether that's America Online or a nonprofit Web site. Join in the conversation, deliver your message in the context of the discussion, and encourage other participants to take an action—whether that means visiting your site or picking up the phone to contact the legislature. And recognize that some forums are more useful than others. If you participate in a forum that feels like a waste of time, trust your hunch: move on.

Now that we've outlined some of the tools that are at your disposal, the next step is to design your campaign. For the purposes of discussion and illustration, let's take two approaches: first, a zero-dollar strategy to advance the ABC Act in Congress; and second, a long-term strategy to help an established organization build a cyberadvocacy presence.

No Frills Advocacy

As an emerging online activist, we'll assume that you have secured access to a computer, a modem, and subscribed with an Internet Service Provider. You have Internet access and an e-mail account.

Defining the Goal

The first step is to determine the goal of your online advocacy campaign. For the purposes of this exercise, our goal is to demonstrate to Congress strong public support for passage of the ABC Act. We've decided to demonstrate this support by generating constituent e-mail to Congress in support of ABC.

Identifying Targets

The second step is to identify your off-line political targets and the online target audience most likely to influence them.

For example, are we focusing on the entire U.S. House and Senate or one chamber only? Do we want to limit our activities to swing voters in the House, or are we interested in generating mass mail, regardless of the stance of the legislator?

If we are working to influence particular swing voters in the House, we will want to consider strategies to target constituents in their own congressional districts. If we are working more broadly to generate e-mail to Congress, we can focus generally on the audience online most likely to support passage of ABC. In our case, we want to generate e-mail to the entire Congress, and we believe parents and voting age women are the primary audience likely to support our position on ABC.

Framing the Issue with an Appealing Message

The third step is to develop an advocacy message to advance your issue—one that is clear and compelling, and which will resonate with your target audience. We select, "Tell Congress to Put Our Children First. Vote Yes on ABC." We develop some talking points on the importance of passing ABC, in easy to understand, user friendly language that reflects the concerns of women and parents.

Researching Available Online Tools

The fourth step is to assess the tools at your disposal for building an online activist community to generate messages to Congress on ABC. We don't have money to build a fancy site, but we do have a personal Web page provided by our Internet Service Provider. We also have access to the services provided on other Web sites. For example, *www.Homestead.com* is one of a number of free Web hosting services that give users free

Web space (in exchange for advertising). *Homestead.com* enables users the ability to add features like chat and online searching to their sites, all with the click and drag of their computer mouse. *www.Geocities.com* also offers Web users a free site. Take a look at the options.

Cyberlobby tools for our online activists are available on *www.Congress.org*. We can add a "Write to Congress" badge to our site (provided free for your use from *www.Congress.org*) that links site visitors to these capabilities, including the ability to help supporters identify their members of Congress and send e-mail on our issue. Or, if we are only interested in reaching the U.S. House of Representatives, we can go to *www.house.gov/writerep*, the House Web site's Write Your Rep capability.

We also have access to online tools to help us promote our issue with the press. By linking to *www.Congress.org*, we can enable our Web site visitors to identify and send personal e-mail to the editors of the key newspapers in their state on the importance of passing the ABC Act.

Help for the Novice Web Designer

Even if you don't know hypertext markup language, the major browsers offer a simple solution: Netscape Communicator's Netscape Composer and Internet Explorer's Frontpage Express. These free tools are called WYSIWYG editors, an acronym for "What You See Is What You Get." WYSIWYGs allow the novice Web designer to create and post text and graphics to a Web site without knowing a stitch of computer code. To find the WYSIWYG, simply launch your Web browser, Netscape Communicator or Internet Explorer. In Netscape Communicator, select "Communicator" from the file menu and click on "Composer." In Internet Explorer, click on the file menu and select "Edit with Microsoft Frontpage Editor." If you don't see these items in the selection, you will need to download a new—and complete—version of the browser.

If you're looking for additional technical solutions presented in an easy to follow tutorial format, visit *www.hotwired.com/webmonkey*, a great source for learning about Web design and development.

Building an E-mail List

We also have a personal rolodex of friends, family, and colleagues to whom we can send e-mail urging support for passage of ABC. We can use this rolodex as the basis of an e-mail list. *PC World Magazine's* June 1999 edition recommended EGroups (*www.egroups.com*) as a top source to help Web users create and administer public and private e-mail lists—at no cost. Check around the Web for available sources. There are many providers.

Assembling Your Online Campaign

After assessing the options, the fifth step is to decide which tools we'll use and get to work assembling the mechanics of our campaign. If you have limited time and energy, keep things simple: create a user friendly Web site that clearly defines the issue of ABC and gives people a way to take action—right there online. And, in every case, build an e-mail list.

Promoting Your Campaign

The sixth step is to promote our campaign to friends and colleagues, the online community, and the press. We have research tools available on the Web to help us identify existing e-mail lists, forums, and chats that directly and indirectly address our issue. Using the search engines, we can find sources—such as *www.liszt.com*—that can connect us to other Internet users who care about the ABC Act. Since the ABC Act has been in the news lately, we can take our issue to many of the current events forums on the major Web sites and the online venues of major newspapers. In addition, we've found a number of public e-mail lists that reach our target audiences, parents and women.

Post the alert message to relevant Web sites, newsgroups, and e-mail lists you've identified. Bring your issue to the chatrooms and forums that are discussing this issue or similar topics of interest. Send out e-mail alert messages to your friends and colleagues. Include in your posts a link to your Web site and the cyberlobby tools to take action. If there is a bill number, use it. Ask potential supporters to send you a copy of the messages they transmit so that you can keep track of the success of your campaign. And, this is key: recruit your friends and online supporters as volunteers for the campaign. With minimal effort, your friends and colleagues can help you by passing your message on to their friends. One simple strategy to encourage forwarding is to add an e-mail signature to your own e-mail messages that contain a link to your site, your campaign message, and a request to pass it on. Tell people how they can subscribe to—and get off—your e-mail list.

Write a simple press release to distribute to your local and statewide newspapers, and local radio and television stations on the issue of ABC and your cybercampaign. Include your Web site address, e-mail address, and daytime phone numbers in the release.

Link your site to other Web sites covering the ABC Act. In return, request that the Webmasters of those key sites link to your site, as well. As John Aravosis' experience with the Matthew Shepard Web site demonstrated, persuasion may not be necessary if your campaign is generating significant traffic on an issue.

From *www.register-it.com*, Netscape Netcenter's Web Site Garage, would-be advocates can register their Web sites with 11 search engines at no cost. Many Web users rely on search engines to find the information they're seeking.

Before submitting your site to the search engines, be sure to give each page a title that describes completely and accurately the site content (this is how the search engines will find the information we are advancing online). Various Web marketers recommend strategies for keeping your site high on the search engine list. Among them: use letters from the beginning of the alphabet at the start of the title for each page (for example, ABC Act Status Report, not Status Report on the ABC Act). Identify the keywords that best describe the contents of the site and the focus of your advocacy effort. An activist who is searching the Web will type in a few key phrases to seek out information on this issue. What might those phrases include? Embed key words into the pages of your site using metatags, a type of programming code that the search engines will recognize.

Keeping the Campaign Alive

Now that you've laid the groundwork, the seventh step is to keep the Internet fires burning on your issue. Keep your site fresh and your content current. Things to mention: How many messages have been sent to your political targets on the issue?

Has Congress taken any action on ABC? Use the site to inform, educate, and mobilize potential supporters. As soon as you have relevant news to report, send a follow-up e-mail to your cybertroops. And urge them to pass it on!

Reporting Success

The eighth step is to notify your political targets and the media of your success. Send the e-mail messages, and then tell your political targets you've sent them. In the case of "Censure and Move On," the campaign arranged to hand deliver the petitions to members of Congress in their home districts. If a personal visit isn't feasible, recruit a volunteer to help call the offices of your key targets with the message. The point is: they know you know. And that makes your campaign more difficult to ignore.

The press is very interested in hearing about the progress of successful online advocacy campaigns. Send a follow-up release notifying them of the number of e-mail messages sent, phone calls generated, and so on. Be factual and concise, but do let them know.

Recognizing Supporters

The ninth step is to thank the people who contribute to your campaign. If it's feasible, send a quick e-mail of thanks to those who have sent messages from your site. If you can't send individual expressions of gratitude, send a message to the entire e-mail list. Express your thanks via the Web site—but don't name names. It's important to protect the privacy of your online army.

ncing Results

enth step is to report the results. Perhaps you won the w... *le* issue—ABC passes both chambers and the president signs the bill into law. Tell your activists. Perhaps Congress voted the wrong way or took no action at all—let them know. Perhaps your targets voted right—but the vote went down all the same—bring it to your activists' attention.

It's the last step, and it may seem tedious. But, it's important. In part, informing your network of the end result is a matter of courtesy. Providing this information also produces other direct benefits, for your cause and your long-term strategy as an online activist. Remember the expression, "We'll remember in November?" That's what political action is all about: electing people who will represent your interests. And, if our friends and colleagues online know that Congressman Smith voted down ABC—even after they asked him to vote for it— they will remember. Count on it. In politics, every legislative session is a new day—your new day to pass ABC.

Building Organizational Capacity

Organizations moving their agendas online follow a similar process to the one outlined in these pages. Additionally, they need to consider other, more complex, issues. There is, for example, the issue of infrastructure: A free, 10 megabyte Web site is fine for an individual. It is insufficient to house the site of a national advocacy organization. There is the issue of resources: an individual may be able to deal with online advertising on their Web site in exchange for access to certain free tools. An organization may have a problem with *de facto* product endorsements and prefer to spend money to get advertisement-free use of tools for their site. And beyond the mechanics, who will staff the campaign, keep the content fresh, find the activists, keep the audience engaged, and move the message? There is the issue of "branding" your organization as a player in the online community, establishing goodwill online, and promoting your site as a living, breathing extension of your organization.

Organizations need to consider online advocacy in the context of the larger organizational mission. Enacting one piece of legislation—the ABC Act—requires a different level of commitment than achieving a mission—world peace, for example. If the advocacy goal is large and long-term in scope, the organization needs to think beyond the flash campaign. Make a requisite commitment of resources and consider online advocacy for the long haul.

Organizational structure can dramatically impact the scope and "look" of online advocacy. Nonprofits, for example, face different online challenges and opportunities than their colleagues in the corporate arena. Associations generally focus their attention on getting volunteer members to participate in achieving a goal. Corporations don't have the luxury of volunteer members to support their advocacy work. They have employees, who may or may not appreciate the opportunity to advocate on issues supported by their employer.

Assessing Current Capabilities

Because no two organizations are exactly alike, there is no one "right answer" or single strategy that will help every organization to achieve its advocacy objectives online. Nevertheless, it's worthwhile to study and learn from the success of others. It's also helpful to spend some time looking "inward." What is the organization's current capacity to play in the online arena? What resources and tools are now in place to conduct advocacy online? How does this compare with your organizational friends and foes in the advocacy world? To be successful, what building blocks must the organization put in place?

Regardless of the operating structure or the intricacies of the organizational goal, the time to prepare for a crisis is before you face one. The time to build an online network of supporters is before you need one. The right time to improve your online infrastructure is before it fails you. Below are some of the key questions an organization should consider in preparing to build an online advocacy presence to support its mission or to assess the program now in place.

Technical

☐ Does your organization have a Web site now and is the infrastructure in place to handle the rapid growth associated with a successful issue-advocacy campaign?

☐ Does your organization provide Internet access for the key staff in your organization?

☐ Do your technical staff use technology to achieve your organizational mission? Or, is there a disconnect between the public affairs and technical staff?

☐ Does your organization's Web site provide advocacy information now; and, if so, do site visitors visit these pages?

☐ How easy is it for users to find advocacy information on your site? Does your home page link visitors to advocacy information?

❒ Does your Web site enable users to e-mail or fax Congress and the administration? Can users e-mail or fax state legislatures and governors from your site?

❒ Does your site provide the opportunity for users to join an e-mail activist list to promote your issues?

❒ What other interactive tools—forums, bulletin boards, and so on—does your site offer online activists?

❒ Has your organization developed an Intranet to give staff efficient access to internal documents and relevant information on the Internet? Do you have access?

❒ Does your organization devote a section of its Intranet site to advocacy—legislative or political?

❒ Does your Intranet enable users to e-mail Congress and state legislatures?

❒ Is your site valued as an important resource by your members and clients?

Financial

❒ Does your budget include resources to purchase hardware and software and to update both periodically?

❒ Does your budget include resources to hire staff and/or consultants to develop and manage a sustained online advocacy program?

❒ Does your budget provide for staff training to keep up with technological changes, including resources for magazine subscriptions and conferences?

❒ Does your budget include resources for advertising—print, direct mail, online advertising—to support recruitment of online activists, to market the Web site generally and advocacy content specifically, and so on?

Promotion

❏ Do you have a recruitment plan for collecting e-mail addresses of potential online activists and building an e-mail list to support your issues?

❏ Do you have an advertising and marketing plan in place to promote your Web presence (and advocacy area) and e-mail activist list?

❏ Have you integrated your e-mail activist list with other grassroots communications programs?

Staffing

❏ Does your organization have trained staff to devote to a cyberadvocacy campaign?

❏ If not, does your organization have cyberadvocacy consultants on-hand to build and support the growth of your program?

These questions provide a framework for viewing the organization's readiness to conduct advocacy in cyberspace.

Building the Plan

The next step is to build the online advocacy plan, based on the organization's overall advocacy objectives. The plan should take advantage of the organization's strengths and outline strategies to address its deficiencies, based on a realistic assessment of the available resources. For example, $2,000 won't buy a lot of Web site infrastructure. It will, however, pay for cyberlobby tools. A plan that calls for daily updated legislative content without a requisite staffing commitment is bound to fall short. Build a plan that is measurable, achievable, and within your means.

As part of this planning process, consider the strategies that will move your program forward for the long-term. What strategies can you employ to recruit online activists? What content can you provide on your Web site that will make it a valuable resource for the public, or your Intranet site a useful tool for your employees? How can you use existing publications and materials to promote your Web site and e-mail activist list?

Hired Hands

While cyberadvocacy is a relatively new field, it isn't necessary to go it alone online. As with every profession, there are consulting firms whose business it is to help clients use the Net as a tool for political advocacy. It's important to choose wisely, however, and seek out the help of specialists who have hands-on experience designing, building, and executing cyberadvocacy campaigns. When we formed our own consulting firm, *e*-advocates, we did so to address a gap in the marketplace: a lack of professional experts with first-hand knowledge of public affairs work and Congress, and with demonstrated experience using the Internet to organize and mobilize grassroots constituencies online.

How can consultants help you to move an advocacy agenda online? It depends on their experience and expertise. A good consultant can help you with a range of services, from advocacy site design, community building, cyberactivist recruitment and retention, to training and organizational capacity building. They can help you to recruit and motivate online activists and build cybercommunities to carry your message to Congress, the White House, state legislatures—wherever and whenever help is needed.

An online consultant can assess your current Web site's effectiveness as an advocacy tool and offer suggestions to help you improve the interface and its functionality for grassroots activism and mobilization. In addition, your online professional should have skills to help you develop specialized issue-advocacy Web sites, as the need arises, and have the knowledge of the latest tools for conducting cyberadvocacy campaigns, from online petitions to "tell a friend" campaign features.

Your online consultant should be a fluent communicator—in the cyber medium. A consultant should be able to help you frame and target your advocacy message for online audiences and off-line results. Based on your needs and objectives, he or she can help you develop content for your Web site, craft e-mail newsletters targeted to your activist base, and draft action alerts that generate results.

An online professional should also have the skills to help you design a high-impact online advertising campaign that maximizes your advertising dollars and extends your reach online. Ask for samples of past advertising campaigns developed by the firm, and for the results they generated.

A professional can also take your case to online communities, speak out for your issue in chatrooms and forums, newsgroups and bulletin boards. A consultant should have the skills to help your organization develop an online relationship with your target audience and establish you as the organizational leader on your issues. As a key element in your organizing strategy, a consultant can also help you recruit e-mail activists for your cause and build and manage an e-mail list that achieves results for your issue.

To empower your entire staff to use the Internet effectively for advocacy, a consultant should be able to help you design training and capacity-building programs that advance your organizational mission in the Digital Age.

The Net Effect

Building an online advocacy program is a serious undertaking and a long-term commitment. It isn't a job for the receptionist or the office intern. This is your business—your face to the public and to your elected representatives. Put the resources in place—including the staff and consulting expertise—and build a program and a presence of which you can be proud.

As this book has highlighted, the Internet is changing the political landscape as we know it. Successful organizations like the ACLU and activists like Joan Blades and Wes Boyd are already learning how to tap its potential. And those public affairs professionals and organizations that lag behind, or ignore the Internet entirely, will do so at their peril. More importantly, they will imperil their issues in the Digital Age.

The Net effect is changing everything around us: family life, communities, careers, economies, media, politics. It is changing organizations, the way we work, and the way we organize. The stories revealed in these pages are just the beginning. The next chapters have yet to be written. They will be created by a new generation of activists and organizations, the cyberpioneers. It is our hope that they will be helped by the lessons and information we have shared here. Good planning and safe journey, cyberpioneers.

Style Sheet for Cyberadvocacy

With two writers writing about the nexus of Internet and politics, there ended up being three or more ways to use or coin words to describe this new landscape. With the help of Tim Yoder, we have arrived at decisions on how best to spell and use these terms. We have included a usage guide for others writing on this new subject.

applet
> Web pages can be made more interactive with a Java *applet*.

ASCII file
> An *ASCII file* can be read by any computer.

bandwidth
> The greater the *bandwidth*, the faster the connection.

bookmark
> Be sure to *bookmark* www.congress.org.

bulletin board
> When planning your flash campaign, you'll want to consider posting messages to pertinent *bulletin boards*.

CD-ROM
> It won't be long before DVD replaces the *CD-ROM* as the industry standard.

chat room
> When planning your flash campaign, you'll want to consider setting up a *chat room*.

compact disc
> You can play a *compact disc* on a CD-ROM drive.

Control key *(all key names are capitalized followed by a lower-case "key")*

cyber
> *Cyber* is a prefix and gets no hyphen.

cyberactivist
> Anyone can be a *cyberactivist*.

cybercampaign

Strategy and a good message are key to winning a *cybercampaign*.

cyberentrepreneurs

Bob Hansan is a *cyberentrepreneur*.

cyberevent

No event is complete, unless it is also a *cyberevent*.

cyberlobbyist

Anybody with Internet access can be a *cyberlobbyist*.

cyberpioneers

Blazing a trail into the next century is a new breed of *cyberpioneers*.

cyberpolitics

Whoever understands *cyberpolitics* the best will have the upperhand in the next election.

cyberspace

The frontier of the next century will be *cyberspace*.

desktop

The appearance of your *desktop* is customizable.

dial-up

With the growth of DSL and cable, *dial-up* Internet access has gotten cheaper.

Dial-Up Networking

Working from home is made possible by *Dial-Up Networking*.

digital

Computers are *digital* machines.

Digital Age

Many people argue that the *Digital Age* began with the success of the personal computer.

disk cache
The speed of your computer is affected by your *disk cache*.

disk drive
Most computers have at least two types of *disk drives*.

domain name
Campaigns often register several *domain names* as a way to protect themselves from parody sites.

drag-and-drop
It is easier to demonstrate how to *drag-and-drop* than explain it with words.

e-commerce
As *e-commerce*, or electronic commerce, becomes a bigger part of the economy, Congress will undoubtedly look for new ways to tax the consumer.

electronic mail
Easily surpassing snail mail in ease of use is *electronic mail*.

e-mail
Many offices cannot function without *e-mail*.

e-mail address
Making an *e-mail address* will be as common as having a phone number.

e-zine
Many *e-zines* are designed to complement their print versions.

FAQ
A Frequently Asked Questions, or *FAQ*, page is a useful way to educate your Web site visitors.

file server
A simple way to share files in an office is to have a dedicated *file server*.

File Transfer Protocol *(FTP)*

A quick way to send files is to use a *File Transfer Protocol* (FTP) program.

flash campaign

A *flash campaign* is a short-lived, issue specific effort to influence Congress or public opinion.

floppy disk

A cheap and easy way to transport files is by *floppy disk.*

Gopher

The *Gopher* system predates the World Wide Web.

grassroots

Some people argue the real work of shaping public policy is done on a *grassroots* level.

hard drive

Backing up your *hard drive* is crucial if you use it to store important documents.

home page

Your *home page* is your best chance to make a good impression and retain visitors.

home PC

The *home PC* market is booming.

HTML

With the advent of graphical web design, *HTML* is becoming less important.

hyperlink

Your mouse pointer will change shape or color by passing it over a *hyperlink.*

hypertext

A novel can be interactive if written in *hypertext.*

Independent Counsel

An *Independent Counsel* is appointed by the Attorney General.

information superhighway

The *information superhighway* is the Internet.

Internet

The *Internet* has revolutionized the dispersion of information.

Internet advocacy

Cyberconsulting firms such as *e*-advocates specialize in *Internet advocacy.*

Internet democracy

Internet democracy is changing the way Washington works.

Internet radio

Rather than hurting broadcast radio, *Internet radio* is helping many smaller stations.

Internet-based

More and more data entry is becoming *Internet-based.*

Intranet

You can purchase Capitol Advantage's services for your company *Intranet.*

IRC

The Internet Relay Chat, or *IRC*, is a live chat system developed in the 1980s by Jarkko Oikarinen.

ISP

America Online is the largest *ISP*, or Internet Service Provider.

log off

If you forget to *log off*, your computer will do it for you after a period of time.

log on

The first thing you do in the morning is *log on* the network.

log out

If you forget to *log out*, you may incur unnecessary charges.

micro *(prefix, no hyphen)*

Many cyberentrepreneurs have become wealthy designing *micro*processors.

Morse code

A vital part of America's westward expansion was the invention of *Morse code.*

multimedia

The House Press Gallery contains an assortment of *multimedia* devices.

newsgroup

There are *newsgroups* covering virtually every topic.

off-line

My computer was *off-line* this morning.

on-air discussion/callers

A hazard of live radio is the unpredictable nature of *on-air callers.*

online

You have to go *online* to access the World Wide Web.

pop-up menu/window/etc.

The list of files is in the *pop-up menu.*

pull-down menu

Choose your option from the *pull-down menu.*

screen saver

Why should I use a *screen saver?*

software

WordPerfect is a *software* package.

streaming

The *streaming* video of C-SPAN is available through their Web site.

Thomas Web site

Legislation can be found at the *Thomas Web site.*

USENET

I like the newsgroups in *USENET.*

username

You must have a *username* and password to log on the computer.

Web

The *Web* has millions of users.

Web address

The *Web address* for the President is www.whitehouse.gov.

Web browser

Netscape and Explorer are popular *Web browsers.*

Web mail

I use Netscape for my *Web mail.*

Web page

Please visit my Web page at www.e-advocates.com.

Web server

Their *Web server* was down for an hour last night.

Web site

Please visit our *Web site* at www.congress.org.

Webmaster

If you have problems with the Web site, please contact the *Webmaster.*

window

I have a *window* open for word processing.

Windows 95/98, etc.

Did you upgrade your operating system to *Windows 98?*

World Wide Web

The *World Wide Web* is expanding each day.

Index

M

N

O

Office of the Independent Counsel 8, 9, 11
OMB Watch 154
Open Secrets 143

P

Parks, Rosa 2
Pataki, George 140
PC World Magazine 160
Pentagon 70
Philadelphia Inquirer 101
Politicker 62
PoliticsNow 58, 59
PoliticsOnline 60
PoliticsUSA 58, 59

R

RealNetworks 42
Richards, Michelle 95
Rockefeller, John D., IV 96, 100
Rockefeller, Nelson 58
Rogan, Jim 48
Roll Call 48-52, 54, 66-68
Roll Call Online 67
Rooney, Kevin 51, 57, 66-69, 77
Roosevelt, Franklin D. 15, 41
Rush, Bobby L. 18

S

Salon 49
San Francisco 129
San Francisco Chronicle 52
San Jose 129
Santorum, Rick 100
Save the E-Rate Coalition 95, 97, 100-102, 105-107, 154, 155
SBC Communications 95, 97, 105
Schneider, Troy 59
Schools and Libraries Corporation 102
search engines 161, 162

V

W

About the Authors

Daniel Bennett, *recently named to the "Federal 100" by Federal Computer Week, is an Internet communications developer, writer, and technology policy expert who has consulted for Congress, media organizations, nonprofits, and corporations. Bennett drafted the Government Paperwork Elimination Act of 1998. He has earned critical acclaim as a columnist for the National Journal's Cloakroom Web site.*

Pam Fielding *is a policy writer and cyberlobbyist who has spent more than 10 years working in the association arena. She designed and launched one of the most successful cyberadvocacy programs in the country. Her online campaigns have been covered by Campaigns & Elections magazine, USA Today Online, New York Times on the Web and numerous other publications. Fielding has conducted presentations on Internet advocacy for many associations, advocacy organizations, and trade groups.*

www.e-advocates.com
info@e-advocates.com

ORDER FORM

Please send_____copies of *The Net Effect: How Cyberadvocacy is Changing the Political Landscape* at $24.95 per book.

(VA residents/business add 4.5% sales tax)

Send us your order or call toll free:

e-advocates

P.O. Box 2018
Merrifield, VA 22116-2018
703-289-9636
800-659-8708

Name _____

Organization _____

Address _____

_____

City/State/ZIP _____

Phone _____ Fax _____

e-mail _____

p Enclosed is a check payable to **e-advocates**
p Bill this order to:

_____Visa_____Mastercard_____Am/Ex

Card# _____

Expiration date _____

Name on Card _____

Signature _____